MODESZENE SCHWEIZ
THE SWISS FASHION SCENE

WILD THING

MUSEUM FÜR GESTALTUNG ZÜRICH / KARIN GIMMI, CHRISTOPH HEFTI (HRSG. / EDS.)

SCHEIDEGGER & SPIESS

GRUSSWORT

Vor genau 70 Jahren zeigte das Zürcher Kunstgewerbemuseum (das heutige Museum für Gestaltung Zürich) die Ausstellung *Sechshundert Jahre Zürcher Seide.* Damals wussten in der Limmatstadt noch fast alle, dass Zürich eine stolze Seidenstadt war, deren Anfänge bis ins Mittelalter zurückgehen und die im 19. Jahrhundert zu der nach Lyon wichtigsten Produzentin modischer Kleiderstoffe aufstieg.

Inzwischen sind die letzten Seidenwebereien im Kanton geschlossen, ihre reichen Archivbestände lagern in den Depots des Landesmuseums und des Staatsarchivs. Aber die Zürcherische Seidenindustrie Gesellschaft (ZSIG), den Verband der Branche, gibt es noch heute, und sie ist in der glücklichen Lage, Projekte mit Bezug zur Zürcher Seidentradition fördern zu können. Dazu zählt selbstverständlich das Modeschaffen, denn Seide und Mode gingen schon immer Hand in Hand.

In der vorliegenden Begleitpublikation zur Ausstellung *Wild Thing — Modeszene Schweiz* erklärt mein Vorstandskollege Ronald Weisbrod, wie wir uns in den letzten Jahrzehnten für Mode in der Schweiz eingesetzt haben. Zunächst im Kontext der *Gwand,* später durch die *Mode Suisse.* Dass das Museum für Gestaltung Zürich zahlreiche Modeschaffende für seine Ausstellung ausgewählt hat, die wir in früheren Stadien ihrer Karriere bereits haben fördern dürfen, freut uns ganz besonders.

THOMAS ISLER, Präsident Zürcherische Seidenindustrie Gesellschaft (ZSIG)

A WORD OF WELCOME

It was exactly seventy years ago that the Zürcher Kunstgewerbemuseum (today the Museum für Gestaltung Zürich) presented the exhibition *Six Hundred Years of Zurich Silk.* At the time, Zurich's inhabitants still knew it as a proud city of silk, a tradition going back to the Middle Ages, which by the nineteenth century had made it second only to Lyon as a producer of fashionable dress fabrics.

In the meantime, the last silk-weaving mills in the canton have closed down, and their rich archival holdings are today stored in the National Museum and the State Archives. But the Zurich Silk Association (Zürcherische Seidenindustrie Gesellschaft, ZSIG) still exists and is fortunate to be able to promote projects addressing Zurich's silk heritage. This of course includes fashion design, because silk and fashion have always gone hand in hand.

In this publication accompanying the exhibition *Wild Thing — The Swiss Fashion Scene,* my colleague on the board, Ronald Weisbrod, explains how we have been championing Swiss fashion over the past decades, first within the *Gwand* and later through *Mode Suisse.* We are particularly pleased that, for this exhibition, the Museum für Gestaltung Zürich has selected a number of fashion designers whom we were able to support in earlier stages of their careers.

THOMAS ISLER, President of the Zurich Silk Association (ZSIG)

PRIMO — PRINT IN MOTION

In diesem Buch lassen sich alle schwarz-weissen Videostills—in der Legende als VIDEO gekennzeichnet—mit der App PRIMO Print in motion in Bewegung versetzen. Laden Sie die App herunter und scannen Sie den Buchumschlag. Der zugehörige Videostream startet, sobald die Kamera auf ein Videostill gerichtet ist, und lässt sich auch im Vollbildmodus betrachten.

PRIMO — PRINT IN MOTION

In this book all printed black-and-white video stills—marked as VIDEO in the caption—can be set in motion with the PRIMO Print in motion app. Download the app and scan the book cover. The associated video stream starts as soon as the camera is pointed at a video still. If desired, switch to full-screen mode.

 APPLE STORE

 GOOGLE PLAY

KARIN GIMMI

IT'S A WILD THING — Die aktuelle Schweizer Modelandschaft ist überraschend bunt und vielfältig. Offensichtlich sind ausreichend Motivation und die Voraussetzungen vorhanden, Bekleidung als etwas essenziell Kreatives und gesellschaftlich höchst Relevantes aufzufassen. Das gilt für Designerinnen und Designer wie für die Käuferschaft. Anders ist nicht zu erklären, weshalb neben wenigen grösseren in den letzten Jahren zahlreiche kleinere Labels von sich reden machen. Wer versucht, von der lebendigen Szene ein verbindliches Bild zu erhalten, begegnet allerdings der Schwierigkeit, dass alles in Bewegung ist. Was noch gestern Gültigkeit hatte, steht unter Umständen bereits heute ausser Diskussion. Das gehört grundsätzlich zur Mode. In der Schweiz ist das Terrain, auf dem diese steht, wenig stabil. Im Geschäft mit der Mode finanziell erfolgreich zu sein, bleibt eine grosse Herausforderung. Jedes Jahr nehmen junge Studienabgängerinnen und -abgänger sowie etabliertere Designerinnen und Designer dieses Wagnis von Neuem in Kauf und beweisen damit eindrücklich das schöpferische Potenzial der Schweizer Modeszene.

IT'S A WILD THING

Switzerland's current fashion landscape is surprisingly multicolored and diverse. Motivation abounds, and the prevailing conditions are conducive to regarding clothing design as an essential creative enterprise that is highly relevant to society. This view is evidently held by both designers and consumers, as there's simply no other way to explain why so many smaller labels have made such a splash in recent years alongside the few major players. However, any attempt to paint a reliable picture of the lively scene is difficult, because everything is constantly in motion here. What was still cutting edge just yesterday may today already be a thing of the past. Of course, that's all part of fashion. In Switzerland, the ground on which it stands is not very stable. Achieving any kind of financial success in the fashion business is still a daunting challenge. And yet, every year, young fashion school graduates as well as established designers try to make a go of it, in the process demonstrating the astounding creative potential of the Swiss fashion scene.

MODE IM MUSEUM

Gemessen am Tempo in der Modewelt agieren eine Ausstellung oder eine Publikation meist im langsamen Modus. Sie halten etwas fest, das im Fluss ist. Eine flüchtige Momentaufnahme, ein spontaner Schnappschuss wird da zum Stillleben. Das birgt natürlich das Risiko, bereits bei Eröffnung oder Erscheinen nicht auf dem neusten Stand zu sein. Zusätzlich sieht sich Mode im Museum damit konfrontiert, dass sie sich grundsätzlich erst am Körper der Menschen, die sie tragen, und in bestimmten Kontexten realisiert. Bis vor wenigen Jahren gelangten deshalb mehrheitlich vergangene Moden ins Museum und auch dies meist nur in Häusern und Institutionen, die sich auf Mode- oder Kostümgeschichte spezialisiert haben. Das Museum of Modern Art in New York mag ein Beispiel für diese Zurückhaltung sein. Die Designdisziplin Mode fand dort erst kürzlich ihren Platz im Ausstellungsprogramm.[1]

Das scheint sich neuerdings zu ändern. Denn sowohl bei Veranstaltern wie auch beim Publikum gilt Mode, vor allem ihre zeitgenössische Ausformung, als äusserst faszinierende und attraktive Materie.[2] Auch grosse Kunstmuseen widmen sich ihr vermehrt. Wie unlängst im Kunsthaus Zürich wird dabei der historisch verbürgte Dialog von Mode und Kunst neu thematisiert.[3] Die Befürchtung, dem Gegenstand Mode in Form von Ausstellungen und Katalogen nicht gerecht werden zu können, ist seit einigen Jahren einer wahren Lust und dem Bedürfnis gewichen, die Fantasien und Träume, die soziokulturellen Realitäten und Identifikationsmomente, die Mode eben auch liefert, öffentlich zur Diskussion zu stellen. Zugleich erfährt Mode durch die museale Präsentation eine Aufwertung. Sobald sie als Konsumgut aus ihrem Gebrauchszusammenhang gerissen wird, verliert sie den Status als reine Ware.[4]

HAUTE COUTURE, KONFEKTION, MODE

Die heutige Schweizer Modeszene ist ein jüngeres Phänomen. Noch in den 1950er-Jahren

[1] Paola Antonelli (Hrsg.): *Items. Is Fashion Modern?* New York 2017, vgl. insbesondere das Kapitel «Who's Afraid of Fashion», S. 16.
[2] Die spektakulärsten Schauen der letzten Jahre galten zunächst dem Werk einzelner Designerpersönlichkeiten. Stellvertretend seien hier *Yohji Yamamoto* (2010 im Victoria & Albert Museum in London), *Alexander McQueen* (2011 im Metropolitan Museum of Art in New York), *Jean-Paul Gaultier* (2015 im Grand Palais in Paris) oder die grosse Dior-Schau (2019 ebenfalls im Victoria & Albert Museum in London) erwähnt.
[3] Cathérine Hug, Christoph Becker (Hrsg.): *Fashion Drive.* Zürich 2019.
[4] Gertrud Lehnert: *Mode. Theorie, Geschichte und Ästhetik einer kulturellen Praxis.* Bielefeld 2013, S. 128.

FASHION IN THE MUSEUM

Measured against the fast pace of fashion, an exhibition or publication usually operates in slow mode. It tries to pin down something that is in flux. A fleeting impression, a spontaneous snapshot becomes a still life. There is of course always the risk of not being quite up to date by the time the opening takes place or the book is released. What's more, fashion really only comes alive on the bodies of the people who wear it and in specific contexts, something that can't readily be recreated in a museum. This is why, until a few years ago, the tendency was to exhibit only fashions from the past, and then almost exclusively in institutions specializing in fashion or costume history. The Museum of Modern Art in New York, for example, did not include the discipline of fashion design in its exhibition program until fairly recently.[1]

But all that seems to be changing. After all, fashion, especially in its contemporary form, is a fascinating and attractive subject for both curators and the public.[2] Even major art museums are now devoting more attention to it. In the process, the historical dialogue between fashion and art is being revisited, for example recently at Kunsthaus Zürich.[3] The fear of not really doing justice to fashion with static exhibitions and catalogues has over the past several years given way to a genuine desire and a felt need to publicly discuss the fantasies and dreams, the sociocultural realities, and moments of identification that fashion can provide. And fashion, in turn, takes on greater perceived value when presented in a museum. Wrested from its context as a consumer product, it becomes more than a mere commodity.[4]

HAUTE COUTURE, READY-TO-WEAR, FASHION

Today's Swiss fashion scene is quite a recent phenomenon. As late as the 1950s, the term fashion was still mostly associated with the big haute couture houses in Paris, with women as the main clientele. Fashion meant Dior, Balenciaga,

[1] *Items. Is Fashion Modern?*, ed. Paola Antonelli, Museum of Modern Art, New York, 2017, cf. esp. Antonelli, "Who's Afraid of Fashion," p. 16.
[2] The most spectacular shows of recent years were initially devoted to the work of individual designers. Prime examples are *Yohji Yamamoto* at the Victoria & Albert Museum in London in 2010, *Alexander McQueen* at the Metropolitan Museum of Art in New York in 2011, *Jean-Paul Gaultier* at the Grand Palais in Paris in 2015, and the big Dior show mounted by the Victoria & Albert Museum in 2019.
[3] *Fashion Drive*, eds. Cathérine Hug and Christoph Becker, Kunsthaus Zurich, 2019.
[4] Gertrud Lehnert, *Mode. Theorie, Geschichte und Ästhetik einer kulturellen Praxis*, transcript Verlag, Bielefeld, 2013, p. 128.

[5] Birgit Littmann: «Elegant, aber immer tragbar. Schweizer Damenmode 1950–1970», in: Sigrid Pallmert, Barbara Welter, Beatrice Hirt (Hrsg.), Modedesign Schweiz 1972–1997, Zürich 1997, S. 15.
[6] Zit. nach Gina Bucher (Hrsg.): Female Chic, Zürich 2016, S. 7.

verband man mit dem Begriff Mode mehrheitlich die grossen Haute-Couture-Häuser in Paris, adressiert wurde vornehmlich die Frau. Mode bedeutete Dior, Balenciaga oder Balmain. Zweimal jährlich trafen sich die Einkäuferinnen und Einkäufer der Schweizer Modehäuser an den Schauen in Paris, wo ihnen nicht nur die neuesten Kreationen vorgeführt, sondern auch Lizenzen zum Kopieren der originalen Modelle verkauft wurden. Die eigenen Haute-Couture-Entwürfe sollten zwar elegant wie in Paris, aber zurückhaltend und in Zürich, Genf oder Bern tragbar sein.[5] Bald erfasste der Wandel im Modeverhalten auch die Schweiz. Die exklusive Haute Couture, aufwendig produziert und teuer, entsprach zunehmend weniger den Lebensgewohnheiten der modernen Frau. In den 1960er-Jahren verloren deren verwässerte Konfektionsmodelle auch bei den Schweizerinnen mit hohen Ansprüchen an Stil und Eleganz an Bedeutung. Den (Berufs-)Alltag bestritten die Frauen neu in Fertigkleidung von der Stange. Diese Mode zeigte durchaus zeitgenössische Looks, war von anonymen Schnittmacherinnen und Schnittmachern entworfen und wurde in Kaufhäusern wie Globus oder Modissa verkauft. Die Jugend avancierte zwar zum Vorbild für eine «junge Mode» und die Schweizer Konfektionsindustrie produzierte wirtschaftlich erfolgreich – modisch aber fehlte ihr der nötige Mut.

Erst mit der Gründung des Labels Thema Selection in den frühen 1970er-Jahren kam Bewegung in die Schweizer Modeszene. Ursula Rodel, Katharina Bebié und Sissi Zoebeli zeigten in ihrer Boutique in der Zürcher Altstadt einfach geschnittene Arbeitskleidung und androgyne Outfits für die zeitgenössische Frau. Rodel sagte später rückblickend über die damalige Umbruchstimmung, dass die Mode endlich aufgehört habe, den Frauen zu diktieren, was diese zu tragen hätten. Parallel zur Emanzipationsbewegung seien die Versuche, die Kundin zu manipulieren, fragwürdig geworden. Und der unerträgliche Druck der Konfektionsindustrie habe den schöpferischen Freiraum der Modemacherinnen und Modemacher komplett beschnitten.[6] Als 1974 die amerikanische Vogue enthusiastisch über die Avantgarde-Mode von Thema Selection berichtete,

[5] Birgit Littmann, "Elegant, aber immer tragbar. Schweizer Damenmode 1950–1970," in Modedesign Schweiz 1972–1997, eds. Sigrid Pallmert, Barbara Welter, and Beatrice Hirt, Schweizerisches Landesmuseum, Zurich, 1997, p.15.
[6] Quoted from: Female Chic, ed. Gina Bucher, Edition Patrick Frey, Zurich, 2016, p. 7.

or Balmain. Twice a year, the buyers for Swiss fashion boutiques would meet up at the shows in Paris, where they were not only presented with the latest creations but could also purchase licenses to copy the original designs. Their own haute couture should be just as elegant as what they saw in Paris, but more restrained so that it was wearable in Zurich, Geneva, or Bern.[5] Soon, however, sweeping changes in attitudes toward fashion would make their way to Switzerland as well. Exclusive haute couture, elaborately produced and costly, was less and less appropriate for the lifestyles of modern women. In the 1960s, the popularity of watered-down haute couture began declining even among Swiss women with exacting standards of style and elegance. Women now went about their daily (professional) lives in off-the-rack clothing. The womenswear available from department stores such as Globus and Modissa, though designed by anonymous pattern-makers, offered looks that were thoroughly contemporary. And yet, although youth was now the role model for a "young fashion," and the Swiss ready-to-wear industry was successful in turning out marketable apparel, there was a hesitation to try anything bold or different.

It was not until the Thema Selection label was founded in the early 1970s that things began to liven up on the Swiss fashion scene. In their boutique in Zurich's Old Town, Ursula Rodel, Katharina Bebié, and Sissi Zoebeli showed simply cut work clothes and androgynous outfits for the contemporary woman. Rodel would later say, looking back at the fresh spirit that prevailed at the time, that fashion had finally stopped dictating to women what they should wear. In the days of the women's liberation movement, any attempt to manipulate the customer had become suspect. At the same time, the unbearable pressure of the ready-to-wear industry had utterly squashed fashion designers' creative freedom.[6] When, in 1974, the US edition of Vogue magazine featured an enthusiastic article on the avant-garde fashions created by Thema Selection, the label's star began to rise. This was thanks in no small part to the legendary fashion shows the brand staged at unusual locations, with a well-known Zurich prostitute as model and a spoken song

stellte sich der Erfolg des Labels ein. Nicht zuletzt wegen der legendären Modeschauen, die an ungewöhnlichen Orten mit einer stadtbekannten Prostituierten als Model und einem Sprechgesang des Künstlers Dieter Meier[7] aufgeführt wurden, galten die drei Gründerinnen von Thema Selection in der Presse als «die schönen Wilden»[8]. Sie läuteten mit ihrem Label den Aufbruch in ein zeitgemässes Verständnis von Mode in der Schweiz ein, das bis heute Gültigkeit hat: Einfach kombinierbare Basics unterstreichen das neue Selbstverständnis der Frauen, Inspirationen von der Strasse und von Subkulturen wie auch der Anspruch an eine hochwertige Verarbeitung fliessen in die Kollektionen ein. Mode wird als Teil des gesellschaftlichen Systems verstanden.

AUF UND NEBEN DEM INTERNATIONALEN LAUFSTEG

In den Jahrzehnten seit der Gründung der frühen Schweizer Modemarken Thema Selection und Lataa Style, später Pink Flamingo oder Annex,[9]

hat sich einiges getan. Nicht nur die Zahl der Designerinnen und Designer, der Fotografinnen und Fotografen, der Labels, Vertriebskanäle und -plattformen hat sich erhöht, auch der gestalterische Reichtum ist wesentlich grösser geworden. Gleich geblieben ist der Anspruch, etwas Eigenständiges zu entwickeln, das sich komplementär verhält zur Mode, wie sie sich in den grossen Zentren Paris, London, Mailand oder New York abspielt. Denn was dort zählt – die schnellen saisonalen Rhythmen oder die Finanzkraft von grossen Häusern – ist hier praktisch inexistent. In der Schweiz fehlen Hollywood, internationale Fashion Weeks oder eine Grossindustrie. Mit Ausnahme weniger Marken wird dem Gros der Schweizer Modeszene von einer internationalen Käuferschaft keine Beachtung geschenkt. Wie kann Schweizer Mode dennoch funktionieren?

Neben wenigen etablierten Marken erproben viele kleinere Labels, Kollektive und junge Absolventinnen und Absolventen von Modeschulen ihr Potenzial. Mit einer unverwechselbaren gestalterischen Sprache und Erfindergeist positionieren sie sich auf eigene Faust in Berlin,

[7] Sigrid Pallmert: «Schweizer Modedesign–Annäherung an ein Phänomen», in: Sigrid Pallmert, Barbara Welter, Beatrice Hirt (Hrsg.): *Modedesign Schweiz 1972–1997.* Zürich 1997, S. 49.
[8] Gina Bucher: «Time for Us to Get Started Too», in: dies. (Hrsg.): *Female Chic.* Zürich 2016. S. 32.
[9] Vgl. dazu Sigrid Pallmert: «Schweizer Modedesign–Annäherung an ein Phänomen», in: Sigrid Pallmert, Barbara Welter, Beatrice Hirt (Hrsg.): *Modedesign Schweiz 1972–1997.* Zürich 1997, S. 46ff.

by the artist Dieter Meier[7] as accompaniment. The press referred to the three founders of Thema Selection as "the beautiful wild things."[8] With their label, they heralded a contemporary take on fashion in Switzerland that still prevails today, with collections featuring easily combinable basics that enhance women's new self-image, inspirations from streetwear and subcultures, and high-quality workmanship. Fashion is understood here as part of the social system.

ON AND BEYOND THE INTERNATIONAL CATWALK

In the decades since the founding of the early Swiss fashion brands Thema Selection and Lataa Style, and later Pink Flamingo and Annex,[9] much has changed. Not only are there more designers and photographers as well as labels, distribution channels, and platforms in Switzerland these days; the creative diversity is also much greater. What is still the same, though, is the aspiration to develop something independent and

yet complementary to what is happening in the major fashion hubs of Paris, London, Milan, and New York. Because what counts there – the fast-paced seasonal rhythms and the financial clout of the big fashion houses – is practically nonexistent here. Switzerland has no Hollywood, no international fashion weeks, no large industry. With the exception of a few brands, international clients pay little heed to the fashion scene here. So how can Swiss fashion still function?

Alongside the handful of established brands, many smaller labels, collectives, and young fashion school graduates are currently testing the waters. Equipped with a design language all their own and an inventive spirit, they are setting up shop on their own in Berlin, juggling in the Paris fashion circus, or establishing intelligent business systems in Switzerland. Integration into the international fashion business is neither guaranteed nor out of the question. That the global fashion world today, with its rampant depletion of resources, is feeling the pressure to justify itself opens up new prospects for the Swiss fashion scene. People everywhere

[7] Sigrid Pallmert, "Schweizer Modedesign–Annäherung an ein Phänomen," in *Modedesign Schweiz 1972–1997,* eds. Sigrid Pallmert, Barbara Welter, and Beatrice Hirt, Schweizerisches Landesmuseum, Zurich, 1997, p. 49.
[8] Gina Bucher, "Time for Us to Get Started Too," in *Female Chic,* Edition Patrick Frey, Zurich, 2016, p. 32.
[9] Cf. Sigrid Pallmert, "Schweizer Modedesign–Annäherung an ein Phänomen" (see note 7), pp. 46ff.

jonglieren im Pariser Modezirkus mit oder richten in der Schweiz clevere Businesssysteme ein. Der Anschluss an das internationale Geschäft ist dabei weder garantiert noch ausgeschlossen. Dass die globale Mode und ihr Ressourcenverschleiss heute unter grossem Rechtfertigungsdruck stehen, kann der hiesigen Modeszene neue Perspektiven eröffnen. Denn vielerorts wird ein Systemwechsel hin zu mehr lokaler Produktion, direktem Verkauf und zum effektiven Bedarf der Kundschaft gefordert.

Die Recherchen zu aktuell käuflichen Kollektionen, Laufstegmodellen, Bildern in den sozialen Medien, Masterkollektionen an Schulen oder zu den Gewinnerinnen und Gewinnern von Designpreisen haben eine erstaunliche Vielfalt interessanter Positionen und Produkte zutage gefördert. Was sie alle auszeichnet, ist der Wille und die Lust, nicht nur tragbare Kleidung, sondern Mode zu machen, und damit in einem scheinbar glamourösen, in Realität aber knochenharten Umfeld zu bestehen. Die engere Auswahl von gut 50 Positionen fiel deshalb nicht leicht, weil die Grenze zwischen vernünftigen, tragbaren Textilien und verrückten Konzepten von Kleidung weder starr

verläuft, noch unverrückbar ist. Sie dürfte über den Moment hinaus zu Diskussionen anregen.

THEMEN UND TENDENZEN

Wir haben, losgelöst von den wechselnden Kollektionen, nach dem Essenziellen einer Marke und den ihr zugrunde liegenden Kerngedanken gesucht. Wir haben Zuordnungen vorgenommen, Gruppierungen erstellt, nach Analogien Ausschau gehalten und dabei vieles wieder verworfen. Das scheinbar wilde Gewirr einzelner Ströme wies erst nach und nach in benennbare Fliessrichtungen, es bildeten sich thematische Terrains oder Inseln heraus. Es sind Themen, die in der Luft liegen, die sich bei Atelierbesuchen und in Gesprächen mit Expertinnen und Experten bestätigten, die nationale Eigenheiten ebenso widerspiegeln wie globale Tendenzen und die sich bei den Labels auf ganz unterschiedliche Art manifestieren. Wir haben diesen Prozess aktiv forciert und dabei den Fokus auf knapp ein Dutzend Schwerpunkte gelegt. Sie sind das

are pushing for system change which includes local production, direct sales, and services tailored to the costumers' individual needs.

Our research on the latest collections, catwalk pieces, images on social media, master's collections at schools, and the winners of design awards revealed an astonishing array of interesting designers and products. What all these designers share is the will and desire to produce not only wearable clothing but fashion, and thus to survive in an environment that, behind its glamorous facade, conceals a tough reality. It was not easy to put together a shortlist of around fifty labels and designers, because the line between sensible, wearable garments and crazy clothing concepts is neither rigid nor unchanging. The selection is thus geared toward stimulating further discussion.

THEMES AND TRENDS

We tried to look beyond the changing collections and discover the quintessence of the respective

brand and the core ideas underlying it. We categorized, created groupings, looked for analogies, and ended up discarding many of our initial ideas. The seemingly wild tangle of individual fashion currents only gradually organized itself into identifiable directions, forming thematic terrains or islands. These are themes that are in the air today, as confirmed on studio visits and in conversations with designers and experts—themes that reflect national Swiss characteristics as well as global trends and that manifest themselves in the labels in very different ways. We actively fostered this process of elimination, narrowing the focus to just under a dozen key areas. They then build the temporary scaffolding on which to hang the wild thing that is Swiss fashion.

In the area we refer to as *Crossing Boundaries*, cultural diversity is writ large. Foreign elements not only exert a general fascination in fashion; they are a matter-of-fact part of the biography and work of some of the designers in the show, who move deftly between the different cultures. Gender issues are also shaping the current social discourse, in both Switzerland and abroad.

temporäre Gerüst, an dem wir das wilde Ding der Schweizer Mode aufhängen.

In jenem Bereich, den wir mit *Über die Grenze* bezeichnen, wird kulturelle Vielfalt grossgeschrieben. Das Andere übt nicht nur generell eine Faszination auf die Mode aus, es ist selbstverständlicher Teil der Biografie und Arbeit einiger Modedesignerinnen und -designer in der Schweiz. Diese bewegen sich gekonnt zwischen den unterschiedlichen Kulturen. Auch Genderfragen prägen nicht nur in der Schweiz den aktuellen gesellschaftlichen Diskurs. In der Mode manifestieren sie sich in Form bestimmter Stereotypen oder *Gender Codes*, die gebrochen, unterlaufen oder unterstrichen werden. Anstelle einer Bipolarität, wie sie noch vor ein paar Jahren in Schnitt, Stoff oder Accessoires vorhanden war, treten heute Genderneutralität, das Fluide oder *Female Power.* Stoff und Schnitt sind seit jeher Kernaspekte in der Mode. Im Kapitel *Stoffkleider* richtet sich der Blick auf eine Mode, deren Look wesentlich aus dem Stoff, insbesondere aus der Kreation eines speziellen Stoffes, entsteht. Die *Textilszene* zeigt das schöpferische Design

hochwertiger Textilien, gleichzeitig liegt hier der Akzent auf der Entwicklung nachhaltiger und technischer Fasern. Einige finden sich in den Kleidern verarbeitet, die zwischen Funktions- und hochmodischer Sportbekleidung changieren und den boomenden *Outdoor*-Markt bedienen. Wie erfinderische und handwerklich raffinierte Schnittkonzepte die Architektur von Kleid und Accessoire bestimmen, wird im Bereich *Schnittmuster* gezeigt. Viele Modekonzepte leben von der Spannung zwischen gestalterischer Reduktion und Freude an Opulenz. *Minimal – Maximal* versammelt Beispiele, bei denen Schnitt, Farbmuster oder die Qualität des Stoffes den einen oder anderen Pol markieren. *Family Matters* nennen wir schliesslich eine Auffassung von Mode, die einen bestimmten Lifestyle zelebriert und die Kundschaft gleichermassen als Teil der sozialen Familie und Basis des Geschäftsmodells versteht. Traditionell eng sind auch die Bande zwischen Kunst und Mode. Ihre zeitgenössische Ausprägung findet sich in den vielen Kollaborationen *Mode × Kunst,* die Kollektionen einmalig und die Kunst modischer machen. Grundsätzlich fällt auf, dass Mode bei vielen Gestalterinnen und

In fashion, they manifest themselves in certain stereotypes, or *Gender Codes*, that may be broken, undermined, or underlined. Instead of the bipolarity that prevailed just a few years ago in terms of cut, fabric, or accessories, gender neutrality is now the order of the day, a new fluidity or *Female Power*. Fabric and cut have always been core aspects of fashion. In the chapter *Fabrics in Clothing*, we look at fashion that derives its look mainly from fabric, and especially from the creation of a special fabric. *The Textile Scene* displays creative designs for high-quality textiles, while also looking at the development of sustainable and technical fibers. Some of these innovative textiles can be found in garments that are both functional and highly fashionable sportswear, catering to the booming *Outdoor* market. The *Patterns* section shows how inventive and technically sophisticated cuts create the architecture of garments and accessories. Many fashion concepts derive their impact from the tension between creative reduction and a delight in opulence. *Minimal — Maximal* brings together examples in which cut, color, pattern, or the quality of the

fabric puts them at one or the other end of the spectrum. Finally, we have chosen the heading *Family Matters* for an attitude toward fashion that celebrates a specific lifestyle and sees the customer equally as part of the family and the basis for the business model. The ties between art and fashion have also traditionally been close. They are currently finding expression in a number of collaborations between *Fashion × Art*, which make collections one-of-a-kind and art more fashionable. Another noticeable trend these days is for fashion designers to reinterpret or repurpose ordinary things in the world around them. The street, sports, and the alpine topography of Switzerland form the backdrop for creative recycling of patterns, materials, colors, and ideas: *Copy, Paste, Refresh*!

THE SWISS FASHION LANDSCAPE

Whereas in the 1970s the textile industry was still a major driving force behind the Swiss fashion scene, today the courses of study at

[10]   Vgl. dazu Elizabeth Fischer: «L'évolution de la formation en Design mode depuis le XXe siècle», in: Bertrand Maréchal (Hrsg.): *Rechercher la Mode.* Genf 2020. S. 166. Die hier zitierte Publikation wird von einer zweiten flankiert, die die Wechselbeziehung zwischen Ausbildung und Forschung ebenso ins Visier nimmt: Luca Marchetti (Hrsg.): *La Mode exposée.* Genf 2020.

Gestaltern aus einer Haltung heraus entsteht, die das Vorhandene und das Gewöhnliche neu oder uminterpretiert. Strasse, Sport oder die alpine Topografie der Schweiz bilden den Fundus für ein kreatives Rezyklieren von Muster, Material, Farben und Ideen: *Copy, Paste, Refresh*!

MODELANDSCHAFT SCHWEIZ

Während in den 1970er-Jahren die Textilwirtschaft der Schweizer Modelandschaft noch massgebliche Impulse verlieh, sind heute die Studiengänge an Fachhochschulen und Universitäten Treiber der aktuellen Modeszene. Neben etlichen kleineren und von privater Hand betriebenen Aus- und Weiterbildungen stecken heute vor allem drei Institutionen das Feld der Mode ab. Diese haben im Laufe der letzten Jahre eine Schärfung ihrer Profile wahrgenommen, sodass sie ganz unterschiedliche Haltungen vertreten, die auch in der Arbeit ihrer Absolventinnen und Absolventen durchdringen. Am Institut Mode-Design der Hochschule für Gestaltung und Kunst

FHNW in Basel wird eine von künstlerischen Praktiken inspirierte und auf ein sehr aktuelles Verständnis von Identität fokussierte Ausbildung angeboten. Die F+F Schule für Kunst und Design Zürich ermöglicht ihren Studierenden ebenfalls eine breite künstlerisch-gestalterische Ausbildung, die von der stets geförderten Zusammenarbeit mit anderen Designabteilungen profitiert. Die HEAD—Genève ihrerseits operiert praxisorientiert und mit Blick auf zeitgenössische gesellschaftliche Fragestellungen. Aktuell ist sie bestrebt, vermehrt Brücken zwischen Theorie und Praxis zu schlagen, um die Studierenden auf einen komplexen globalen Kontext vorzubereiten.[10] Im Vordergrund der verschiedenen Ausbildungen stehen weder Geschichte noch Theorie der Mode, vielmehr geht es um gesellschaftliche Konzepte und Konstrukte. Viele der Modedesignerinnen und -designer, die hier vorgestellt werden, haben eine dieser Schulen durchlaufen.

Ebenso gehören renommierte Ausbildungsstätten in England, Frankreich oder den Niederlanden zur Grundausstattung von Modeschaffenden

[10]   Cf. Elizabeth Fischer, "L'évolution de la formation en Design mode depuis le XXe siècle," in *Rechercher la Mode,* ed. Bertrand Maréchal, HEAD–Genève, 2020, p.166. The publication cited here is flanked by a second one that likewise focuses on the interrelation between education and research: *La Mode exposée,* ed. Luca Marchetti, HEAD–Genève, 2020.
[11]   Cf. www.modesuisse.com.

universities and fashion schools are setting the pace. In addition to a number of smaller, privately run training establishments and further education courses, three institutions in particular are now defining the field of fashion. In the course of the last few years, they have sharpened their profiles, so that they now represent very different attitudes that are also reflected in the graduates' work. Teaching at the Institute of Fashion Design at the FHNW Academy of Art and Design in Basel is inspired by artistic practices and an up-to-the-minute understanding of identity. The F+F School of Art and Design in Zurich likewise offers students a broad artistic and creative education, encouraging collaboration with the other design departments. HEAD—Genève, for its part, puts the emphasis on practical training and examining contemporary social issues. Currently, the school is endeavoring to build more bridges between theory and practice in order to prepare students for a complex global context.[10] In all these study programs, neither history nor the theory of fashion is in the foreground, but rather social concepts and constructs. Many of

the fashion designers presented here graduated from one of the above schools, while others trained at renowned schools in England, France, or the Netherlands.

Apart from the universities and fashion schools, *Mode Suisse*, founded in 2011, forms another important platform for the Swiss fashion scene. Twice a year, the organization puts on a fashion show with affiliated showrooms, as well as sponsoring appearances by Swiss labels in Paris and New York. These efforts have the effect of bringing a whiff of worldly glamor to Switzerland.[11] In addition, the Swiss Federal Office of Culture, which awards annual design prizes, gives fashion design recognition and financial support at the national level. What all these institutions have in common is a vision of fashion as something that happens not only on catwalks or in department stores, not only on the street or in the materials lab, not only in the minds of artists or in Europe's cities, but everywhere.

This common vision is reflected in the superstructure and thematic organization of the exhibition and publication. *Wild Thing* is based

aus der Schweiz. Mit der 2011 gegründeten *Mode Suisse* verfügt die Schweizer Modeszene über eine wichtige Plattform. Zweimal pro Jahr verbreitet sie mit einer Fashion Show, angegliederten Showrooms sowie Auftritten von Schweizer Labels in Paris und New York einen Hauch weltläufigen Glamours.[11] Schliesslich ist auch das Bundesamt für Kultur, das jährlich Designpreise verleiht, bestrebt, das Modeschaffen auf nationaler Ebene anzuerkennen und finanziell zu unterstützen. Allen Institutionen gemein ist eine Perspektive auf die Mode, die sich nicht nur auf den Laufstegen ereignet oder im Warenhaus, nicht nur auf der Strasse oder im Materiallabor, nicht allein im Kopf von Kunstschaffenden oder in der europäischen Stadt—sondern überall.

Die Situation von Ausbildung und Förderung findet im Überbau und in der thematischen Gliederung von Ausstellung und Publikation ihren Niederschlag. *Wild Thing* liegt keine theoretische These, sondern ein handlungsbezogenes Vorgehen zugrunde. Hier treten unterschiedliche Gestalterpositionen sowie Statements von Expertinnen und Experten miteinander in Dialog.

Wild Thing fängt die vielfältigen Stimmen und Standpunkte einer ungezähmten und sich stetig wandelnden Modelandschaft ein. Die Zuordnung der einzelnen Positionen zu den gewählten Themen ist mitnichten exklusiv oder abgeschlossen zu verstehen, im Gegenteil: Sie ist fluid, die Positionen sind mehrdeutig und vielstimmig—ganz wie die Gegenwart.

[11] Vgl. www.modesuisse.com.

not on a theoretical proposition but rather on a pragmatic approach. Different design positions as well as expert statements enter into a dialogue here. *Wild Thing* thus captures the diverse voices and viewpoints of an untamed and ever-changing fashion landscape. Rather than being exclusive or complete, the assignment of individual designers and labels to the selected topics is fluid, because the positions themselves tend to be ambiguous and polyphonic. Just like our present-day world.

SCHNITTMUSTER — Schnittkonzept und -technik sind der Schlüssel zur Schneiderkunst. Couture muss den menschlichen Körper zuerst verstehen und dabei eine Idee entwickeln, was mit einem bestimmten Stoff am Körper passiert. Fällt ein Mantel weit, hat eine Hose einen tiefen Sitz oder sind grosse Taschen aufgesetzt? Der Schnitt bildet die Architektur des Kleides, bestimmt sogar, wie man sich darin bewegt. Während in der Mode Schnittmuster von den einen als normative Vorlage benutzt werden, sind sie für andere Ausgangspunkt für kreative Neuschöpfungen. Eine Jacke oder eine Tasche kann genau deshalb interessant sein, weil wenige präzise Schnitte sie klar definieren.

PATTERNS

The concept and technique of cutting are the key to tailoring. Couturiers must first understand the human body and develop an idea of what happens to a particular fabric on the body. Does a coat have a wide drape, do pants sit low on the hips, or are there large patch pockets? The cut forms the architecture of the garment and even determines how the wearer moves around in it. In fashion, while patterns are used by some as a normative template, for others they form the starting point for creative new directions. A jacket or a bag may be interesting precisely because it is so clearly defined by a few precise cuts.

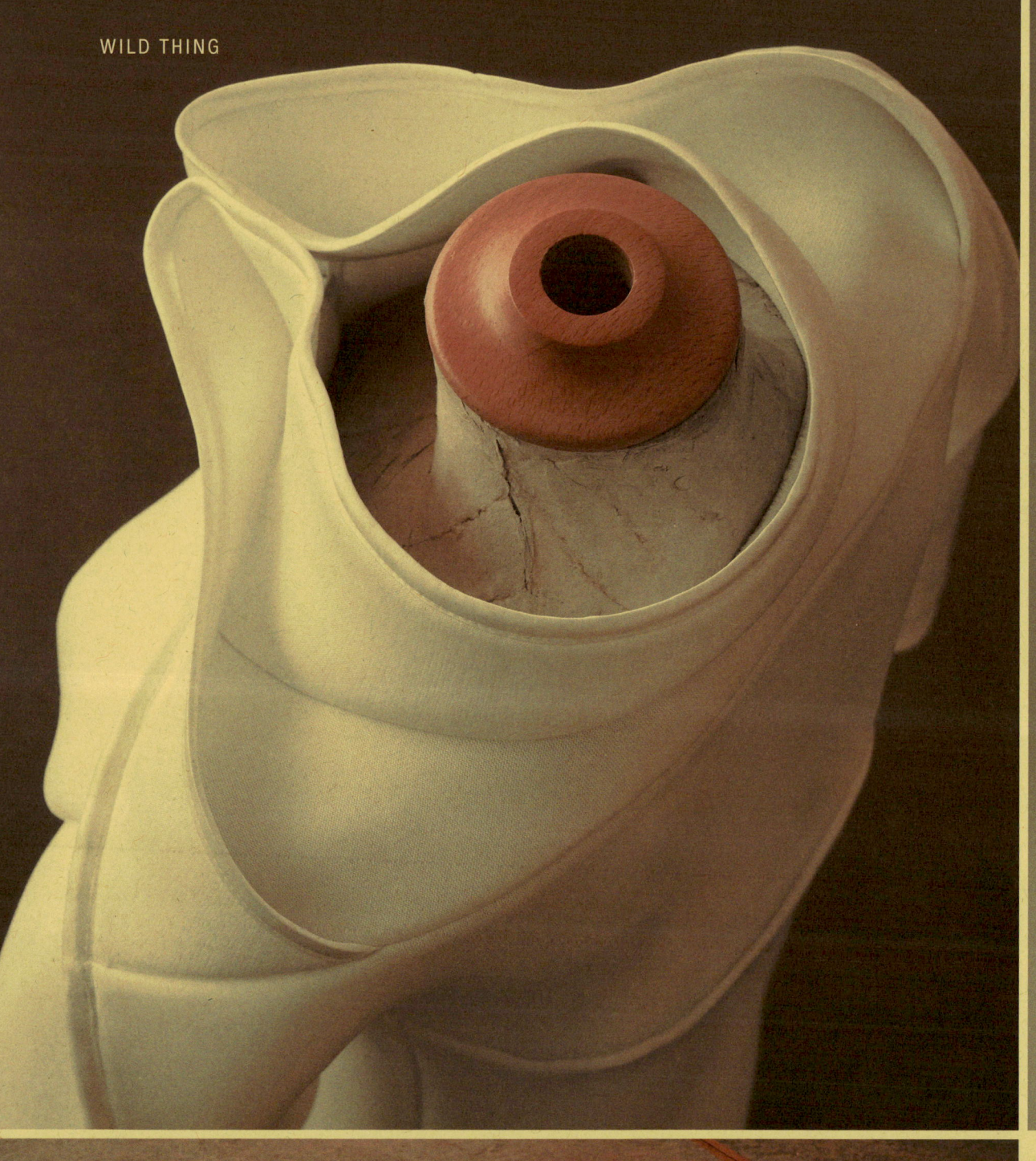

Mantel/Coat ZAK, 2020; Papierfiguren/Paper figures, 2020 |[rechte Seite/right page] Jacke in halbtransparentem Schaumstoffmaterial, Hose WILMA in japanischem Crêpe/Jacket in semi-transparent foam material, trousers WILMA in Japanese crêpe, 2019. Photos: Franz Rindlisbacher

IDA GUT

Ida Gut ist eine Meisterin der Schnittkunst. Die gelernte Schneiderin und Absolventin der Hochschule für Gestaltung und Kunst in Zürich präsentierte 1993 ihre erste Kollektion. Ihre Couture-Stücke sind zeitlos. Sie zeichnen sich durch raffinierte Konstruktionen, hochwertige Materialien und meist beidseitige Tragbarkeit aus. 2020 erhielt sie den Grand Prix Design.

Ida Gut is a master pattern-maker. The trained seamstress and graduate of Zurich School of the Arts presented her first collection in 1993. Her couture pieces are timeless. They are distinguished by sophisticated construction and high-end materials, and are in most cases reversible. Gut was awarded the Grand Prix Design in 2020.

WILD THING

14

COLLECTION 06 — BROT PAIN PANE PAUN, 2020 | [rechte Seite und linke Seite, oben und unten links/ right page and left page, top and bottom left] COLLECTION 05 — METZGETE, 2019. Photos: Moritz Schermbach

COLLECTIVE SWALLOW

Anaïs Marti und Ugo Pecoraio stellen mit Collective Swallow genderneutrale, saisonunabhängige und konzeptuelle Mode her. Nach dem Studium an der Hochschule für Gestaltung und Kunst FHNW in Basel lancierten sie 2017 ihre erste Kollektion. Jede Kollektion thematisiert eine kulinarische Erfahrung, die das Duo in Schnitte, Materialien und Farben übersetzt. Im Herbst 2020 geht es um Brot.

Under their label Collective Swallow, Anaïs Marti and Ugo Pecoraio create gender-neutral, seasonless conceptual fashion. After studying at the FHNW Academy of Art and Design in Basel, they launched their first collection in 2017. Each collection focuses on a specific culinary experience, which the duo translates into cuts, materials, and colors. The theme for Autumn 2020 is bread.

15

Für den Couturier Heiner Wiedemann steht die Form im Zentrum des Entwerfens. Unter dem Namen Heinrich Brambilla entwickelt er Kollektionen, deren Stücke auf Mass bestellt werden können. Wiedemann arbeitet an der Büste, bis Schnitt und Form exakt mit seiner Vorstellung übereinstimmen. Bevorzugtes Material seiner eleganten Entwürfe sind schwere englische (Uniform-)Wollstoffe.

Form is at the center of couturier Heiner Wiedemann's design approach. Under the pseudonym Heinrich Brambilla, he develops elegant collections that are made to measure. Wiedemann works on the dressmaker's dummy until the cut and shape exactly correspond to his vision. He especially likes working with heavy English (uniform) wool.

HEINRICH BRAMBILLA

JEAN & KRULL. 2020 | linke Seite / left page | BETTINA & ERIN. 2020; MAGGOO. 2020. Photos: Lorenz Cugini

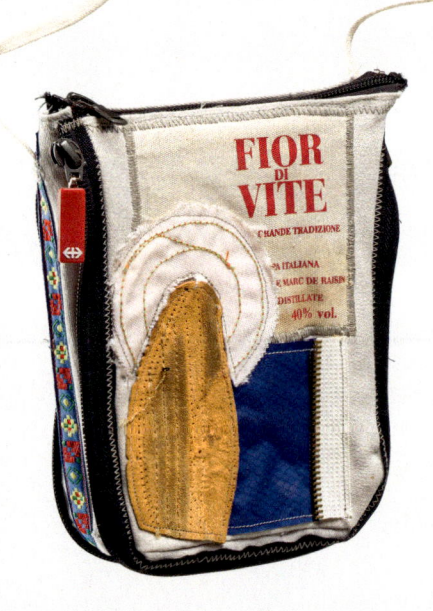

Fabio Prosdocimi verwandelt die gebrauchten Ska-
terschuhe seiner Freunde in einzigartige Taschen.
Brachial schneidet er die Schuhe mit dem Cutter
auseinander und ergänzt sie mit Schnürsenkeln,
Teilen alter Handtaschen oder Stoffresten. Der gelernte Hochbauzeichner studiert Fine Arts an der
Zürcher Hochschule der Künste, das Nähen lernte
er von seiner Grossmutter.

Fabio Prosdocimi transforms his friends' used
skater shoes into unique bags. He brutally cuts
the shoes apart and adds laces, parts of old hand-
bags, or fabric remnants. Prosdocimi trained as a
structural engineering draftsman and now studies fine arts at Zurich University of the Arts; he
learned to sew from his grandmother.

B-BAG (BEER BAG), 2018 | [rechte Seite/right page] COLLAGE, 2018. Photos: Museum für Gestaltung Zürich/Umberto Romito, Ivan Suta

FABIO PROSDOCIMI

FREITAG

Bekannt geworden sind Markus und Daniel Freitag mit der Messenger Bag—1993 von Hand aus gebrauchten Lkw-Planen, Autogurten und Veloschläuchen genäht. Inzwischen verkaufen sie weltweit jährlich rund 700 000 Taschen und Accessoires. Der Schnitt bestimmt Motiv, Farbe und Modell, sodass jede Tasche zum Unikat wird.

Markus and Daniel Freitag became famous with the Messenger Bag they designed in 1993—sewn by hand out of used truck tarpaulins, seatbelts, and bicycle tubes. They now sell some 700,000 bags and accessories worldwide every year. The cut defines type, color, and motif, making each bag unique.

FREITAG BAG DESIGN, 2013. Photo: Joël Tettamanti

MODE × KUNST — Zwischen Kunst und Mode existieren seit jeher enge Bande. Malerei, Fotografie, Film, Musik oder Tanz sind wichtige Inspirationsquellen. Vielerorts hat die freie Kunst bereits während des Modestudiums einen hohen Stellenwert inne. Denn auch Mode soll — vorerst ohne wirtschaftlichen Druck — Regeln brechen, Grenzen ausloten und damit gesellschaftliche Wirkung entfalten. Kollaborationen machen eine Kollektion einmalig und heben sie damit aus dem saisonalen Rhythmus heraus. Für Kunstschaffende ist die Zusammenarbeit mit Modedesignerinnen und -designern deshalb bereichernd, weil der Zwang zur Anwendung dem künstlerischen Konzept eine neue Dimension und mehr Resonanz verleiht.

FASHION × ART

Art and fashion have always been closely allied. Designers derive inspiration from painting, photography, film, music, or dance. At many fashion schools, the fine arts play an important role in studies. After all, fashion, too, should initially be free from commercial pressure so that it can break rules, push boundaries, and have an impact on society. Artistic collaborations make a collection unique and elevate it above the usual seasonal rhythm. And for artists, working with fashion designers is enriching, because real-life application lends the artistic concept a new dimension and greater resonance.

«Die Mode liebt den Intellekt der Kunst, und die Kunst liebt die Vergänglichkeit, die Oberflächlichkeit und das Frivole der Mode.»

"Fashion loves the intellect of art, and art loves the transience, the superficiality, and the frivolity of fashion."

VIDEO — Michelle Nicol im Gespräch mit / in conversation with Christoph Hefti, 10/2020, 4 MIN.

MICHELLE NICOL

«Kunst und Mode standen schon immer in einem sehr engen Austausch. Man denke nur an Yves Saint Laurent, der in den 1960er-Jahren das Mondrian-Kleid entworfen hat. Kunst und Mode flirten miteinander. Die Mode liebt den Intellekt der Kunst, und die Kunst liebt die Vergänglichkeit, die Oberflächlichkeit und das Frivole der Mode. Wenn ein grosses Modehaus mit einem bekannten Künstler zusammenspannt, geht es auch um Marketing. Ist die Zusammenarbeit allerdings nicht authentisch, wird sie nicht funktionieren.

Kunst und Mode wurden gleichermassen demokratisiert. Die kreativen Felder sind für die Lebensqualität der Menschen bedeutender geworden. Die Erkenntnis, dass es wichtig ist, wie man wohnt, mit welchen Dingen man sich umgibt, ist ins Bewusstsein sehr vieler Menschen gerückt.

Wofür die Mode in der Kunst steht oder wie sie eingesetzt wird, kann man nicht generalisieren. Oft wird Mode als Readymade verwendet. Der Künstler nimmt ein Paar glamouröse Stiefel eines bekannten Brand, das wiederum für etwas Bestimmtes steht, und arbeitet es in das Kunstwerk ein. Die Stiefel haben dann nicht mehr dieselbe Funktion, nicht mehr dieselbe Bedeutung. Sie stehen jetzt für Schönheit, für Frivolität, für Oberfläche. Oder auch für ein weibliches Territorium, wenn es Damenstiefel mit hohen Absätzen sind: eine weibliche Sprache, die in die männliche Kunstwelt der Moderne eingearbeitet wird.»

MICHELLE NICOL studierte Kunst- und Filmwissenschaft. 2001 gründete sie zusammen mit Rudolf Schürmann die Branding- und PR-Agentur Neutral. Sie berät international tätige Unternehmen in den Bereichen Kunst, Architektur, Mode und Design bei strategischen Neuausrichtungen oder in der Kommunikation.

"There has always been a very close exchange between art and fashion. Just think of Yves Saint Laurent, for example, who designed the Mondrian dress in the 1960s. Art and fashion flirt with each other. Fashion loves the intellect of art, and art loves the transience, the superficiality, and the frivolity of fashion. When a big fashion house teams up with a well-known artist, it is also about marketing. But if the collaboration is not authentic, it will not work.

You could say that both art and fashion have been democratized. The creative fields have grown more important for people's quality of life. Many people have become aware of the importance of how you live and what items you surround yourself with.

What fashion represents in art, or how it is used, is not something you can generalize. But fashion is often used as a 'ready-made': i.e., the artist takes a pair of glamorous high-heeled boots from a well-known brand, which represents something specific in itself, and incorporates them into a work of art. The boots then no longer have the same purpose, the same significance. They now stand for beauty, for frivolity, for surface—or also for a female territory, if they are women's boots with high heels. A female language, which is incorporated into the male art world of modernism."

MICHELLE NICOL studied art history and film science. In 2001 she founded the branding and PR agency Neutral together with Rudolf Schürmann. She advises globally active companies in the fields of art, architecture, fashion, and design on strategic realignment and communications.

Video: Museum für Gestaltung Zürich. Produktion/Production: schwarzpictures.com, Zürich

Der Modedesigner Julian Zigerli studierte an der Akademie der Künste in Berlin, bevor er 2011 in Zürich sein eigenes Label gründete. Künstlerkollaborationen sind ein zentrales Merkmal seiner Entwürfe. 2014 arbeitete er mit der Künstlerin Katharina Grosse zusammen, die seiner Kollektion durch ihre Sprayarbeiten einen einzigartigen Charakter verlieh.

Julian Zigerli studied fashion design at Berlin University of the Arts before founding his own label in 2011 in Zurich. Artistic collaborations are the hallmarks of his designs. In 2014, he undertook a project with the artist Katharina Grosse, who gave his collection a unique touch with her spray-painting.

JULIAN ZIGERLI
KATHARINA GROSSE

AT THE END OF THE WORLD TO THE LEFT. SS14, 2013. Photos: [linke Seite und rechte Seite, von oben nach unten/left page and right page, from top to bottom] Laurent Burst | [rechte Seite/right page] Amanda Camenisch

E

WILD THING

Für seine Herbstkollektion 2018 wandte sich Julian Zigerli dem Fotografen und Künstler Walter Pfeiffer zu. In der Kollektion *Bold is my favorite color* zieren Pfeiffers Fotos von nackten Männerkörpern Zigerlis Kleiderentwürfe. Als Runway für die Modeschau diente die Gasse am Zürcher Rindermarkt vor Zigerlis Laden.

For his Autumn 2018 collection, Julian Zigerli worked with the photographer and artist Walter Pfeiffer. In the collection, entitled "Bold is my favorite color," Pfeiffer's photos of nude male bodies adorn Zigerli's dress designs. The runway for the fashion show was the Rindermarkt alley outside Zigerli's Zurich shop.

JULIAN ZIGERLI ×
WALTER PFEIFFER

Anstelle einer konventionellen Show präsentierte Julian Zigerli 2018 seine Frühjahrskollektion in Form einer performativen Installation. In *Threesome* verschmilzt Zigerlis Kollektion mit der Malerei von Manon Wertenbroek und den Objekten von Christopher Füllemann. Mode, Malerei und Skulptur praktizieren einen «flotten Dreier».

Instead of a conventional fashion show, Julian Zigerli presented his Spring 2018 collection as a performative installation. In "Threesome," Zigerli's collection melds with a painting by Manon Wertenbroek and objects created by Christopher Füllemann. Fashion, painting, and sculpture embark on an artistic "ménage à trois."

THREESOME. SS18. 2017. Photos: Manon Wertenbroek

JULIAN ZIGERLI ×
MANON WERTENBROEK ×
CHRISTOPHER FÜLLEMANN

JULIA SEEMANN ×
JEAN-VINCENT SIMONET

Yantan Ministry & GIL for IN BLOOM. 2020. Photo: Jean-Vincent Simonet. | linke Seite/left page| Zarah for IN BLOOM. 2020. Photos: Steffen Grap
Yantan Ministry & GIL for IN BLOOM. 2020. Zarah & Johannes for IN BLOOM. 2020. Photos: Steffen Grap

Nach ihrem Modestudium an der Hochschule für Gestaltung und Kunst FHNW in Basel wurde Julia Seemann 2015 direkt auf den Laufsteg der New York Fashion Week katapultiert. Für Seemann ist die Zusammenarbeit mit anderen Künstlern essenziell. Das Werk von Jean-Vincent Simonet bildet den Ausgangspunkt für die aktuelle Kollektion und ein Performance-Projekt mit dem Musikerduo Yantan Ministry & GIL.

After fashion studies at the FHNW Academy of Art and Design in Basel, Julia Seemann was catapulted directly onto the catwalk at New York Fashion Week in 2015. For Seemann, collaboration with other artists is essential. Jean-Vincent Simonet's oeuvre forms the springboard for her latest collection and a performance project with the music duo Yantan Ministry & GIL.

29

In Jean-Vincent Simonets Werk gehen analoge Bilder, digitale Techniken, Collage und Montage fliessend ineinander über. Das Projekt «In Bloom» übersetzt die sinnlichen Eindrücke seiner Begegnungen mit Tokio und Osaka in hypnotisierende Bilder und ist Basis für die Kollaboration mit Julia Seemann. Simonet machte 2014 den Bachelor in Fotografie an der ECAL und lebt heute in Paris und Zürich.

In Jean-Vincent Simonet's oeuvre, analog images, digital techniques, collage, and montage merge fluidly. The project *In Bloom* translates the sensuous impressions of his encounters in Tokyo and Osaka into hypnotic images and is the basis for his collaboration with Julia Seemann. In 2014, Simonet graduated with a bachelor's degree in photography from ECAL / University of Art and Design Lausanne. He lives in Paris and Zurich.

30   JEAN-VINCENT SIMONET

HIGHWAY, 2020, 60 × 80 cm. Tintenstrahldruck auf Plastikfolie, im Diasec-Verfahren auf Acryl montiert / Inkjet print on plastic foil, mounted on Diasec under acrylic

STOFFKLEIDER—Bestimmt der Stoff das Kleid oder ist es der Schnitt, die Farbe? Modedesignerinnen und -designer treffen diese Entscheidung. Sie spannen mit der Stoffdesignerin, dem Stoffdesigner oder einer Textilfirma zusammen—oder sie machen den Stoff gleich in eigener Regie und definieren damit den Look ihrer Kollektion. Das gestalterische Spektrum der Labels ist gross: Stoffreste und alte Glasperlen bilden den Ausgangspunkt einer glamourösen Upcycling-Couture, Experimente mit flüssigem Kunstharz oder tradierte Strohflechttechniken werden bemüht. Gewagte Strickereien, raffinierte Plissee- und Färbetechniken und von Kunstschaffenden entworfene Stoffbilder kreieren hier die Mode und damit das Kleid.

FABRICS IN CLOTHING

Does the fabric make the dress, or is it more the cut or color? This is up to the fashion designers, who work with fabric designers or textile producers to achieve the desired effect. Or they may even make fabric themselves and use it to define the look of their collection. The labels cover a broad creative spectrum: in one case, fabric remnants and old glass beads inspire glamorous upcycled couture, while other designers experiment with liquid synthetic resin or traditional basket-weaving techniques. For some labels, bold knitwear, sophisticated pleating and dyeing techniques, or fabric prints designed by artists create the fashion and thus the clothes.

«Textildesign und Modedesign sind wie zwei Schwestern, die ohne einander nicht existieren können.»

"Textile design and fashion design are like two sisters who cannot exist without each other."

VIDEO — Moritz Ahrens-Pohle im Gespräch mit / in conversation with Christoph Hefti, 10/2020, 4 MIN.

MORITZ AHRENS-POHLE

«Die gängigsten Macharten, um Textilien herzustellen, sind Weben, Stricken, Sticken und Wirken. Das sind die textilen Flächen, die uns im Alltag am meisten umgeben. Darüber hinaus gibt es zum Beispiel noch das Flechten und das Tufting zur Herstellung von Fleecen oder Filzen. Heute können textile Flächen auch mittels eines 3D-Druckers erzeugt werden. Man kann die Textilien ausrüsten und damit Einfluss nehmen auf die Beschaffenheit der Fläche, auf Dichte, Glanz, Wasserdurchlässigkeit und Feuerbeständigkeit. Man kann sie härten oder weicher machen.

Es gibt sicherlich Grenzen, in erster Linie technischer Natur oder durch die Eigenschaften, die das Material mitbringt. Aber sie sind für die Textilindustrie und die Branche immer auch ein Anreiz. Dann erst fängt die richtige Arbeit an, das Tüfteln, das Austricksen und Überwinden der Grenze. Man sollte auch ein Bewusstsein dafür entwickeln, wann es um die eigene Idee geht und wo die Kopie anfängt. Und natürlich gibt es in der Textilherstellung auch moralische Grenzen, zum Beispiel in Bezug auf die Nachhaltigkeit, auf Produktionsstätten, Herstellungsprozesse oder Chemikalien, die man heute nicht mehr verwenden kann.

Der Stoff bestimmt immer das Kleidungsstück. Es ist deshalb wichtig, dass der Modedesigner von Beginn an eng mit dem Schnittgestalter und der Fertigung zusammenarbeitet. Der Schnittgestalter ist gar nicht in der Lage, einen gerechten Schnitt zu entwerfen, ohne das Material zu kennen. Textildesign und Modedesign sind wie zwei Schwestern, die ohne einander nicht existieren können. Sie bedingen einander. Es ist schade, dass die beiden Disziplinen immer ganz klar voneinander getrennt werden. Denn selbstverständlich vermischen sie sich.»

MORITZ AHRENS-POHLE studierte Produkt-, Textil- und Modedesign in Hamburg und erwarb 2016 einen MBA in Handelsmanagement. Er hatte unterschiedliche Positionen bei renommierten Labels wie Vivienne Westwood und Hussein Chalayan in London inne. Seit 2018 ist er Kollektionsmanager bei Jakob Schlaepfer in St. Gallen.

"The most common methods of making textiles are, of course, weaving, knitting, embroidery, and tapestry. These are the textile surfaces that surround us most in everyday life. Beyond that, of course, there is braiding and tufting for the creation of fleeces or felts. Nowadays you can also create textile surfaces using a 3-D printer. Furthermore, you can give them a finish by altering the characteristics of the textile surface—e.g., density, shine, water permeability, or fire resistance. You can make them harder or softer.

There are certainly always limitations, mostly of a technical nature or due to the properties of the material. But for the textile industry, a limitation is always an enticing challenge. Then the real work begins, and you start to tinker and find a way to outsmart your limitations and overcome them. However, it is important to develop an awareness for when an idea is truly your own and when it starts to be a copy. Of course, there are also ethical limitations in textile production—for example, with regard to sustainability. There are manufacturing processes, chemicals, and production facilities that you simply may no longer use today.

The fabric always determines the garment. Therefore it's crucial that the fashion designer works very closely with the pattern designer and the production department from the very beginning. The pattern designer cannot produce a suitable pattern without knowing the fabric. Textile design and fashion design are like two sisters who cannot exist without each other. They depend on each other. It's a pity that these two disciplines are always so clearly separated. Because, of course, the boundaries blur."

MORITZ AHRENS-POHLE studied product, textile, and fashion design in Hamburg and earned an MBA in retail management in 2016. He held various positions with renowned labels such as Vivienne Westwood and Hussein Chalayan in London. Since 2018 he has been collection manager at Jakob Schlaepfer in St. Gallen.

Video: Museum für Gestaltung Zürich. Produktion/Production: schwarzpictures.com, Zürich

SCHIAPARELLI HAUTE COUTURE. AW19/20. Art-Direktion/Artistic director: Daniel Roseberry. Foto/Photo: Thomas Goldblum

CÉCILE FEILCHENFELDT

Die an der Zürcher Hochschule für Gestaltung und Kunst ausgebildete Strickkünstlerin Cécile Feilchenfeldt gewann 2018 den Schweizer Grand Prix Design. In ihrem Pariser Atelier fertigt sie Textilwerke vom kleinen Schmuckstück bis zur Raumskulptur an. Dabei lotet sie konstant die Grenzen des Strickens aus. Ihre Arbeiten inspirieren Kollektionen grosser Modehäuser wie Schiaparelli.

Cécile Feilchenfeldt, a knitting artist who trained at Zurich University of the Arts, won the Swiss Grand Prix Design in 2018. In her Parisian studio, she makes textile works ranging from small pieces of jewelry to sculptures, constantly exploring the limits of knitting. Her works have inspired collections by major fashion houses such as Schiaparelli.

|linke Seite und rechte Seite oben/|left page and right page top| LES FRIVOLITÉS, 2018. Photos: Chaumont-Zaerpour; |rechte Seite unten links/right page, bottom left| FROZEN CHAINS, 2019. Photo: Chaumont-Zaerpour; |rechte Seite unten rechts/right page, bottom right| URETHANE POOL, 2016. Photo: Myriam Ziehli

Vanessa Schindler experimentierte in ihrer Master-Diplomarbeit an der HEAD—Genève mit dem synthetischen Werkstoff Urethan. Die Kollektion, die daraus entstand, wurde 2016 mit dem Prix HEAD Master Mercedes-Benz ausgezeichnet. 2017 gewann sie den Grand Prix des Festival d'Hyères. In ihrem Atelier in Lausanne setzt Schindler aktuell eine Schmuckkollektion aus biobasiertem Giessharz um.

In her master's degree project at HEAD—Genève, Vanessa Schindler experimented with the synthetic material of urethane. The resulting collection was awarded the Prix HEAD Master Mercedes-Benz in 2016. In 2017, she won the Grand Prix at the Festival d'Hyères. Her studio is in Lausanne, where Schindler is currently working on a bio-resin jewelry collection.

VANESSA SCHINDLER

Emma Bruschi schloss 2019 an der HEAD—
Genève ab. Ihre Masterkollektion *Almanach* gewann
im selben Jahr den Prix Master Mercedes-Benz.
Eine Faszination für Techniken der traditionellen Handwerkskunst zeichnet ihre Arbeit aus. Sie
flechtet, webt und strickt natürliche Materiali-
en wie Holz, Stroh oder Weide zu märchenhaften
Kleidungsstücken.

Emma Bruschi graduated from HEAD—Genève in
2019. Her master's degree collection, "Almanach,"
won the Prix Master Mercedes-Benz that same
year. Her work reveals a fascination with traditional crafts techniques. She braids, weaves,
and knits natural materials such as wood, straw,
and willow into fairy tale-like garments.

EMMA BRUSCHI

ALMANACH. 2020. Photos: Cynthia Mai Ammann

02. 4. 9

JULIA HEUER

FUNNY ANIMALS. Kampagne/Campaign AW20. Photo: Edith Karlson. | linke Seite/left page | FUNNY ANIMALS. Lookbook AW20. Photos: Anaïs Horn. 3D: Pastor/Placzek

Seit ihrem Studium des Textildesigns an der Kunstakademie Stuttgart arbeitet Julia Heuer mit einer speziellen japanischen Technik: Sie faltet den Stoff, wickelt ihn um ein Rohr und fixiert alles im Ofen. Im gleichen Prozess wird plissiert. 2017 gründete Heuer ihr Label. Bunte Prints und Plissees kennzeichnen ihren Stil.

After studying textile design at the State Academy of Fine Arts Stuttgart, Julia Heuer has been working with a special Japanese technique: she folds fabric, wraps it around a tube, and fixes everything in the oven. Pleating is done in the same process. She founded her own label, which is known for pleated garments and colorful prints, in 2017.

41

GERMANIER

SS20, 2019. Photos: Alexandre Haefeli

Kévin Germanier studierte an der HEAD—Genève und der Central Saint Martins in London. Eine Anstellung bei Louis Vuitton brachte den Walliser nach Paris, wo er 2018 sein eigenes Label gründete. Das Material für seine glamouröse Couture findet er in Form von Restposten auf Märkten und in Fabriken, die fertigen Kleider präsentiert er an den Pariser Modewochen.

Kévin Germanier studied at HEAD—Genève and Central Saint Martins in London. A job with Louis Vuitton brought him from the Valais region to Paris, where he founded his own label in 2018. For his glamorous couture he uses fabric remnants found at markets and factories, presenting the finished garments at Paris Fashion Week.

43

JULIA SEEMANN ×
RAMON HUNGERBÜHLER

Nach ihrem Modestudium an der Hochschule für Gestaltung und Kunst FHNW in Basel wurde Julia Seemann 2015 direkt auf den Laufsteg der New York Fashion Week katapultiert. Für Seemann ist die Zusammenarbeit mit anderen Kunstschaffenden essenziell. Die Malerei Ramon Hungerbühlers übersetzt Julia Seemann in einen knalligen Print.

After fashion studies at the FHNW Academy of Art and Design in Basel, Julia Seemann was catapulted directly onto the catwalk at New York Fashion Week in 2015. For Seemann, collaboration with other artists is essential. For example, she translated a painting by Ramon Hungerbühler into a striking print.

SI TR GIT, 2016. Photos: Marlen Keller

COPY, PASTE, REFRESH — Verweise und Referenzen sind auch in der zeitgenössischen Mode ein beliebtes Stilmittel. Designerinnen und Designer schauen genau hin, was auf der Strasse, beim Sport oder von der breiten Masse getragen wird. Implizit stellen sie damit das System Mode infrage und dessen Anspruch, ständig Neues zu kreieren. Das französische Designerkollektiv Vetements treibt dieses Prinzip seit einigen Jahren auf die Spitze. Als sich dessen Kreativabteilung 2017 in Zürich niederlässt, hat die Schweizer Modeszene den Trend längst absorbiert. Sie spielt ihn in eigenen Versionen durch: mit Outfits, die gewollt stillos, aber in der Handhabung von Stoff oder Schnitt höchst raffiniert sind.

COPY, PASTE, REFRESH

References and allusions continue to be a popular stylistic device in contemporary fashion. Designers keep close watch over what is being worn on the street, in sports, or by the general public. They implicitly challenge the fashion system and its drive to constantly create something new. The French designer collective Vetements has been taking this principle to extremes for the past several years. By the time its creative department relocated to Zurich in 2017, the Swiss fashion scene had long since taken up the trend. It now plays its own variations on it, with outfits that are deliberately camp or in bad taste but highly refined in their handling of fabric or cut.

Das Modekollektiv aus Bern steht für *Nothing Can Come From Nothing.* NCCFN fokussiert auf Fragen rund um das soziale und ökologische Ungleichgewicht in der Modeindustrie. In Kollaboration mit Marken wie Adidas verwandelt das Label den Abfall der Fast-Fashion-Industrie in neue Stücke, die gleichermassen nachhaltig wie für alle erschwinglich sind.

The name of the fashion collective from Bern stands for "Nothing Can Come From Nothing." NCCFN focuses on issues of social and environmental imbalance in the fashion industry. In collaboration with brands such as Adidas, the collective transforms fast-fashion industry waste into hip new pieces that are both sustainable and affordable for everyone.

[von links nach rechts/from left to right | 1,2 NOTHING CAN COME FROM NOTHING — EX NIHILO NIHIL FIT (NCCFN × adidas), 2020; 3 F.T.P FOR THE PEOPLE (NCCFN × rework), 2020. Photos: Florian Spring]

47

NCCFN

Photo: Jim UZ. Clockwise: PFS Knitting, Attractive Volumetric Knit. Adhesive Texture Sells. Teeth Joins Hook. Oversized Bark. THE UNITED FENCE COMPANY SUES AWS FOR COPYRIGHT INFRINGEMENT. SERIES NO. 6. SS20. SERIES NO. 7. AW20 /21. Photos: James Buntone.

48

Grafiker Matthias Fürst und Modedesignerin Karin Wüthrich kennen sich seit ihrem Studium an der Hochschule für Gestaltung und Kunst FHNW in Basel. Ihr Label kombiniert urbane Sportbekleidung, High-Fashion-Ästhetik und Textilexperimente. 2019 gewannen sie den Design Preis Schweiz. Die charakteristischen Strickstoffe der letzten Kollektionen entstanden lokal in Zusammenarbeit mit der Textil AG, Huttwil.

Graphic artist Matthias Fürst and fashion designer Karin Wüthrich have known each other since their studies at the FHNW Academy of Art and Design in Basel. Their label combines urban sportswear with a high-fashion aesthetic and textile experiments. In 2019, they won the Design Prize Switzerland. The characteristic knitted fabrics of their most recent collections were created locally in cooperation with Textil AG in Huttwil.

AFTER WORK STUDIO

WILD THING

Lukas Wassmann ist Jäger, Zimmermann und Fotograf. Seine künstlerische Ausbildung absolvierte er in Zürich, Berlin und Los Angeles. Sein Portfolio umfasst Mode-, Reportage- und Werbefotografie für Kunden wie Balenciaga, Hermès, Moncler und Ottolinger. Seine Bildsprache setzt auf Gegensätze: Luxuswelt und traditionelle Rituale.

Lukas Wassmann is a hunter, carpenter, and photographer. He completed his artistic education in Zurich, Berlin, and Los Angeles. Today, his portfolio includes fashion, reportage, and advertising photography for clients such as Balenciaga, Hermès, Moncler, and Ottolinger. Wassmann's visual language is based on contrasts: the world of luxury versus traditional rituals.

VETEMENTS × SECHSELÄUTEN, 2018, im Auftrag der Kreativagentur Studio Achermann/on behalf of the creative agency Studio Achermann/Lukas W

LUKAS WASSMANN

Hinter dem 2015 gegründeten Label stehen Christa Bösch und Cosima Gadient. Nach dem Studium an der Hochschule für Gestaltung und Kunst FHNW in Basel zog es die beiden nach Berlin. Konstruktion, Dekonstruktion, Rekonstruktion und Materialexperimente sowie eine bewusst provokante Bildsprache sind ihre Markenzeichen. Ihre Kollektionen präsentieren sie an den Pariser Modewochen.

This label was founded in 2015 by Christa Bösch and Cosima Gadient. After their studies at the FHNW Academy of Art and Design in Basel, the two moved to Berlin. Construction, deconstruction, reconstruction, and material experiments, as well as a deliberately provocative visual language, are their trademarks. They present their collections at Paris Fashion Week.

OTTOLINGER

Kampagne/Campaign SS20, 2019. Photo: Mark Asekhame | rechte Seite/right page | Kampagne/Campaign AW19, 2019, Artwork Julien Ceccaldi

Kampagne/ Campaign S/S19, 2018. Photo: Rcto Schmid

GENDER CODES — Mode kann soziale Klasse oder Geschlechtsidentität signalisieren, unterstreichen oder unterlaufen. Wie eine Person sich kleidet, entscheidet in vielen Fällen darüber, mit welchem Geschlecht und in welcher Rolle sie wahrgenommen wird. Das Spiel mit Gender Codes kann in der Mode aber auch den Wunsch nach gesellschaftlicher Veränderung transportieren. Bereits kleine Verschiebungen von traditionell binär kodifizierten Details — Volants oder Puffärmel für den Mann, eine gerade geschnittene Badehose für die Frau — erzeugen Wirkung. Der Mode kommt deshalb die kreative Aufgabe zu, neue Kleidercodes für eine pluralistische Gesellschaft zu definieren.

GENDER CODES

Fashion may signal, underline, or even undermine social class or gender identity. Personal style often determines how gender and role are perceived. But playing with gender codes in fashion can also convey an urge to bring about social change. Even subtle shifts in traditionally binary-coded details — flounces or puffed sleeves for men, straight-cut swimming trunks for women — can have an impact. Fashion is thus tasked with creatively defining new and up-to-date dress codes for a pluralistic society.

ALEXANDRA BACHZETSIS

Als Choreografin und Künstlerin bewegt sich Alexandra Bachzetsis an der Schnittstelle zwischen Tanz und visueller Kunst. Ihre in Museen, Galerien und auf internationalen Bühnen präsentierten Arbeiten hinterfragen Gender-Stereotypen. Kleider – und die Frage, wie sie getragen werden – sind ein wichtiger Bestandteil ihrer Arbeit. Diese Elemente der Performance entstehen in enger Kollaboration mit Stylistinnen und Modedesignerinnen.

As a choreographer and artist, Alexandra Bachzetsis moves between dance and visual art. Her works, presented worldwide in museums, galleries, and theaters, question gender stereotypes. Clothes — and the question of how they are worn — are an important part of her work. These elements of performance are created in close collaboration with stylists and fashion designers.

ESCAPE ACT by Alexandra Bachzetsis, 2018. Photos: Blommers/Schumm

FORBIDDEN DENIMERIES

AW19. Photo: Mikael Vilchez | [rechte Seite im UZS / right page, clockwise] 1: EDITION 20.1. 2020. Photo: Mikael Vilchez; 2–5: AW19. Mode Suisse Edition 16. Photos: Alexander Palacios; 6: SS20. 2019. Photo: Nicolas Schopfer

Ausgangspunkt für die Entwürfe von Mikael Vilchez bildet der Stoff Denim. Für seine Masterkollektion an der HEAD—Genève übersetzt er den Spirit seiner weiblichen Idole in Denim-Variationen für Männer. Aktuell experimentiert das junge Label Forbidden Denimeries mit Printverfahren, nachhaltigem Färben und genderneutralen Silhouetten.

Denim forms the springboard for Mikael Vilchez's designs. For his master's degree collection at HEAD—Genève, he translated the spirit of his female idols into denim variations for men. With his young label Forbidden Denimeries, he is currently experimenting with print processes, sustainable dyeing, and gender-neutral silhouettes.

In Porrentruy betreibt der Jurassier Luka Maurer ein Atelier für hochwertige Prêt-à-porter-Mode. Mit seinem Label Garnison denkt er den dreiteiligen Männeranzug neu. Der HEAD-Absolvent ergänzt klassisches Schneiderhandwerk mit industriellen Techniken. Er rüttelt an Kleidercodes, ohne dabei die etablierten Regeln der Männergarderobe ganz zu brechen.

Luka Maurer from the Jura region runs a studio for high-end prêt-à-porter fashion in Porrentruy. Under his Garnison label, he produces new takes on the men's three-piece suit. The HEAD—Genève graduate augments classical tailoring with industrial techniques. His garments push the limits of dress codes without completely breaking with the established rules for menswear.

LANGEVIN, Trenchcoat, Oktober/October 2020. Photo: Julie Lahoual | [rechte Seite/right page] BERCHÉNY, Hemd aus plissiertem Lycra/Lycra skin pleated shirt, AW17. Photo: Julien Palmilha

GARNISON

AMOK BY SANDRA KURATLE

Mit ihrem Label AMOK gilt die Zürcherin Sandra Kuratle als Vorreiterin der genderneutralen Mode. Sie macht den Männerrock zum Konzept, erstmals 1996 – in der Zeit der Techno-Bewegung – im Rahmen ihrer Diplomarbeit an der Hochschule für Gestaltung und Kunst in Zürich. Inzwischen umfasst das AMOK-Sortiment rund 50 verschiedene Modelle.

Zurich-based Sandra Kuratle is considered a pioneer of gender-neutral fashion with her label AMOK. She has made men's skirts her main concept, initially in her diploma project at Zurich University of the Arts in 1996 — in the days of the techno movement. Today the AMOK range comprises around fifty different designs.

1: STRYPE, Amsterdam Fashion Week, 2003; 2: D-DRUCK, Blickfang, 2005; 3: PART, Amsterdam Fashion Week, 2003; 4: TAGIO, Blickfang, 2005; 5: WERK, Blickfang, 2004; 6: PO, Amsterdam Fashion Week, 2003; 7: JEANS, Blickfang, 2005; 8: SMOKING, Amsterdam Fashion Week, 2003; 9: SMOKING, Amsterdam Fashion Week, 2003; 10: AS, Amsterdam Fashion Week, 2003; 11: ADIDAS, Centre culturel suisse, Paris, 2003. Photos: [Blickfang] Centre culturel suisse/ Rolf Hättiger; [Amsterdam Fashion Week] unbekannt/unknown

Nach dem Master an der Hochschule für Gestaltung und Kunst FHNW in Basel gründete Jacqueline Loekito 2018 ihr eigenes Label. Ihre Looks fokussieren explizit auf das Thema der modischen Gleichstellung der Geschlechter. Loekito propagiert die Farben Rot und Rosa, kreiert grobe Strickware, arbeitet mit Kunstpelz oder verwendet transparente Stoffe. Ihre Vision ist der Unisex-Kleiderschrank.

After completing her master's degree at the FHNW Academy of Art and Design in Basel, Jacqueline Loekito founded her own label in 2018. Her looks explicitly focus on gender equality in fashion. Loekito likes to work with red and pink, coarse knitwear, faux fur, and transparent fabrics. Her vision is a unisex wardrobe.

JACQUELINE LOEKITO

NATHALIE SCHWEIZER

Als leidenschaftliche Schwimmerin weiss Nathalie Schweizer, worauf es beim perfekten Badekleid ankommt. Seit 2011 entwirft die gelernte Schneiderin in Zürich natürlich-elegante Bademode für Frauen. Produziert wird mit hochwertigen Materialien in Norditalien. Die Kunst liegt in den raffinierten Schnittlinien und der Proportionierung des Körpers.

An avid swimmer, Nathalie Schweizer knows just what makes for the perfect swimsuit. Since 2011, the trained seamstress has been designing naturally elegant swimwear for women in her Zurich studio. The swimsuits are made in northern Italy of high-grade materials. Their artfulness lies in their sophisticated cuts and proportions.

FIBA, 2016. Photos: Gerry Amstutz, Zürich

ÜBER DIE GRENZE — Andere Kulturen üben seit je eine Faszination auf das Design von Mode aus. Eine besondere Prägung erfährt dieser Blick auf das Fremde, wenn er mit der persönlichen Biografie des Designers oder der Designerin korrespondiert. Dann bestimmen Wachsstoffe, einem traditionellen Kimono entlehnte Schnitte oder der bewusste Einsatz von Handarbeit nicht bloss eine Kollektion, sondern sie bilden die Identität eines Labels. Dabei kann sowohl der Designprozess als auch das Geschäftsmodell auf verschiedene Kulturen ausgerichtet sein. Für die entsprechende Mode erweist sich der Schritt über die kulturellen Grenzen als kreativer Mehrwert, der sich auch gut vermarkten lässt.

CROSSING BOUNDARIES

Fashion designers have always been fascinated by foreign cultures. This interest becomes even more intriguing when the culture corresponds with the designer's own biography. Waxed fabrics, cuts inspired by a traditional kimono, or the purposeful deployment of a handicraft may then shape not only a collection but the look of a whole label. Both the design process and the business model may be geared toward different cultures. For the corresponding fashion, crossing cultural boundaries can generate marketable creative added value.

WISHING THIS WORLD WILL LAST FOREVER, 2020. Photos: [links/left] Tihana J. Vukic; [rechts/right] Alexancer Palacios | [rechte Seite/right page] SUSPENDED BODIES THAT WILL NEVER FALL, Apparel Collection, 2019. Art direction: Mark Bryan Kenney. Photo: Jean-Vincent Simonet

SUSPENDED BODIES THAT WILL NEVER FALL. Apparel Collection, 2019. Art direction: Mark Bryan Kenney. Photos: Jean-Vincent Simonet

Nach dem Bachelor in Modedesign an der Hochschule für Gestaltung und Kunst FHNW in Basel absolvierte Rafael Kouto den Master in Fashion Matters am Sandberg Instituut in Amsterdam. Der Tessiner mit Wurzeln in Togo spielt mit einer hybriden Mischung aus europäischer und afrikanischer Ästhetik. Die Unikate basieren auf dem Upcycling-Prinzip und entstehen in Zusammenarbeit mit dem Textilverwerter TEXAID.

After earning a bachelor's in fashion design at the FHNW Academy of Art and Design in Basel, Rafael Kouto went on to do a master's degree in Fashion Matters at the Sandberg Instituut in Amsterdam. The designer from Ticino, with roots in Togo, mixes European and African aesthetics. One-of-a-kind garments based on the upcycling principle are produced in cooperation with the textile recycler TEXAID.

POPLIN PROJECT

MAKE WAVES, 2020. Photo: Dan Cermak Photography | rechte Seite/right page | Video: Museum für Gestaltung Züri:h. Produktion/Production: schwarzpictures.com, Zürich (mit Bildern von/with images by Susann Schweizer)

Langjährige Erfahrung in der Modeindustrie und die Begeisterung für westafrikanische Handwerkskunst sind der Schlüssel zu Susann Schweizers Label. Traditionelle Wax Prints oder bunte Batikstoffe kontrastieren einfache Schnitte. Zusammen mit Ateliers in Côte d'Ivoire entsteht jährlich eine Slow-Fashion-Kollektion, verkauft wird in Pop-up-Läden oder online.

Many years of experience in the fashion industry and a love of West African craftsmanship are the keys to Susann Schweizer's label. Simple cuts form a contrast to traditional wax prints and colorful batik fabrics. Schweizer works with studios in Côte d'Ivoire to produce an annual slow-fashion collection, which is sold in pop-up shops and online.

VIDEO — Susann Schweizer im Gespräch mit / in conversation with Christoph Hefti, 10/2020, 5 MIN.

«Poplin Project ist ein sozial engagiertes Slow Fashion Label. Es soll eine nachhaltige Entwicklung in den Bereichen des Kunsthandwerks, der traditionellen Textilien und indigenen Textiltechniken fördern.

Die Inspiration findet wechselseitig statt. Eine Kollektion entsteht letztlich durch die Verschmelzung verschiedener kreativer Ansätze und kultureller Backgrounds. Die Schweiz ist sehr präzis in ihren Designideen und deren Umsetzung. In Westafrika passiert vieles eher spontan.

Eine neue Kollektion wird jeweils vor Ort lanciert, die hiesigen Techniken verbinden sich dann mit meinen Entwurfsideen. Man probiert aus, findet Lösungen, die funktionieren, stellt Prototypen her – und meistens kommt es anders als ursprünglich gedacht, dafür entsteht etwas Neues oder etwas Besseres.

Nachhaltige Projekte können verschiedene Ansatzpunkte haben, Fair Trade ist einer davon. Ich verkaufe die Produkte fast nur direkt, was die Bezahlung besser und die Preise günstiger macht. Dass es keine Zwischenhändler gibt, ist mir wichtig, es gewährleistet die Transparenz.

Um Cultural Appropriation zu vermeiden, braucht es einen respektvollen, transparenten Austausch ohne Machtgefälle und ohne die Dominanz einer Kultur gegenüber der anderen.»

"Poplin Project is a socially engaged slow fashion label. It promotes sustainable development, specifically in the handicraft and textile sector, in traditional textiles, and in indigenous textile techniques.

The inspiration is mutual. A collection is ultimately created through fusion of the different creative approaches and cultural backgrounds. Switzerland is very precise in terms of design ideas and aspects. In West Africa, things happen more spontaneously.

Each new collection is launched on-site; the local techniques are combined with my design ideas. You try out new things, find solutions that work, make prototypes—and usually things turn out differently than originally planned; instead, something new or better has come out of it.

Sustainable projects can have different starting points: fair trade is one of them. I sell my products almost exclusively directly, which allows for better payment and lower prices. The fact that there are no middlemen is an essential aspect for me; it guarantees transparency.

In order to avoid cultural appropriation, a respectful, transparent cross-cultural exchange without an imbalance of power or the dominance of one culture over another is essential."

«KAZU transformiert japanische Kunst und Kultur in zeitgenössische Mode. Die TAN Collection ist wahrscheinlich die authentischste Kreation. *Tan* ist japanisch und bezeichnet eine Stoffrolle, die aus einem etwa 12 Meter langen und 38 Zentimeter breiten Band besteht. Aus einem Tan entsteht ein ganzer Kimono: Der Stoff wird horizontal geschnitten, zweimal für die Ärmel und zweimal für die linke und rechte Hauptseite. Man schneidet nicht in den Stoff, sondern näht die Bahnen der Webkante entlang zusammen, dabei entsteht kaum Abfall.

Japan hat eine alte Tradition des Recyclings. Die Bahnen werden absichtlich nicht zerschnitten, damit der wertvolle Stoff wiederverwendet werden kann. So haben wir uns spezialisiert: Aus auseinandergetrennten Stoffbahnen kreieren wir eigene Modelle, zeitgenössische Kleidung aus ganz alten Unikaten. Die Kimono-Tracht hat etwas wahnsinnig Modernes, einerseits durch den Gedanken des Rezyklierens, andererseits durch ihre Androgynität.»

"KAZU transforms Japanese art and culture into contemporary fashion. The TAN Collection is probably our most authentic creation. Tan means 'fabric roll,' in Japanese. One roll of fabric consists of a strip that is about 12 meters long and 38 centimeters wide. One tan makes an entire kimono: the fabric is cut horizontally, twice for the sleeves and twice for the left and right front and back. You don't cut into the fabric, but simply sew the strips together along the selvage; there is hardly any waste.

Japan has an old tradition of recycling. They deliberately don't cut the panels, so that the precious fabric can be reused again. And so we specialized in creating our own models from unstitched fabric panels — contemporary clothes from very old and unique pieces. The kimono as a traditional costume is in some ways incredibly modern — on the one hand through the idea of recycling, on the other by its androgyny."

VIDEO — Kazu Huggler im Gespräch mit/in conversation with Christoph Hefti, 10/2020, 7 MIN.

UZUME/GÖTTIN DES TANZES. 2019. Photo: Christian Schnur |[linke Seite/left page] Video: Museum für Gestaltung Zürich. Produktion/Production: schwarzpictures.com, Zürich

KAZU

In Zürich und Tokio aufgewachsen, studierte Kazu Huggler Modedesign an der Central Saint Martins in London. Ihr kultureller Hintergrund prägt die Identität ihres Labels. Aus traditionellen japanischen Kimonostoffen entstehen moderne Einzelstücke, Couture- oder Prêt-à-porter-Kollektionen. Ihr Zürcher Atelier ist gleichzeitig Showroom und Produktionsstätte.

After growing up in Zurich and Tokyo, Kazu Huggler studied fashion design at Central Saint Martins in London. Her cultural background informs her label's identity. Traditional Japanese kimono fabrics are transformed into modern one-of-a-kind pieces as well as couture and prêt-à-porter collections. The designer's Zurich studio is both showroom and production site.

TAN COLLECTION before & after [oben/top] AYA Dress, 2020; Sommerkimono/Summer kimono, ca. 1920; [unten/bottom] Sommerkimono/Summer kimono, ca. 1940; AYA Dress, 2020. Photos: Christian Schnur

TEXTILSZENE — Die Textilbranche ist in ganz unterschiedlichen Szenen aktiv, Bekleidung und Mode stehen gegenwärtig nicht an erster Stelle. Viele Betriebe haben sich auf nachhaltige Fasern und technologische Industriegewebe spezialisiert. Statt in die kurzen Zyklen der Mode investieren sie in die langlebigen Produkte einer Kreislaufwirtschaft. Das Entwerfen von Textilien erfordert Flexibilität, da ein Stoff noch kein Endprodukt ist. Textildesignerinnen und -designer arbeiten nicht nur für die Industrie, sondern auch als selbstständige Unternehmerinnen und Unternehmer. Sie tüfteln an neuen Bildsprachen oder innovativen Materialien herum und produzieren auch in Eigenregie: Vorhänge, Foulards, Teppiche oder Kunst.

THE TEXTILE SCENE

The textile industry is active on a number of fronts, and clothing and fashion are not its main focus at the moment. Many companies are specializing instead in sustainable fibers and high-tech industrial fabrics. Rather than relying on fashion with its short product cycles, they are investing in the long-lived products of a circular economy. Designing textiles calls for flexibility, because a fabric is not yet an end product. Textile designers thus work not only for industry but also as independent entrepreneurs, experimenting with new visual languages or innovative materials and producing their own creations, for example curtains, silk scarves, carpets, or art.

«Die Liaison zwischen Mode und Textil mag in der Kulturgeschichte mal vertrauter, mal distanzierter sein, die Abhängigkeit voneinander aber war immer existenziell.»

"The liaison between fashion and textiles is a part of cultural history that may sometimes seem familiar and at other times more distant, but their interdependence has always been existential."

VIDEO — Evelyne Roth im Gespräch mit / in conversation with Karin Gimmi, 11/2020, 6 MIN.

EVELYNE ROTH

EVELYNE ROTH

«Die Liaison zwischen Mode und Textil mag in der Kulturgeschichte mal vertrauter, mal distanzierter sein, die Abhängigkeit voneinander aber war immer existenziell: ohne Textil keine Mode, ohne Mode keine umgestaltende Textilindustrie. Dass wir sie als zwei verschiedene Designdisziplinen verstehen, ist längst überholt. Wer heute Produkte entwickelt, forscht am Material, entwirft Oberflächen und handelt zirkulär. Gestalten bedeutet, Verantwortung zu übernehmen. Der Fokus der Verantwortung ist immer im Wandel und eng mit den soziokulturellen Themen der jeweiligen Zeit verknüpft. Das kann visuell mal ausgefallen extrovertiert, bewusst und radikal unmodisch oder zeitlos sein. Letzteres ist ein Phänomen, das modischer natürlich nicht sein könnte. Die Frage, ob Schweizer Textildesign national und international eine Zukunft hat, hängt davon ab, wie die heutigen Player auf die relevanten Themen der Gegenwart reagieren und ihre Firmen- wie Produktestruktur weiterentwickeln. Aus der Forschung wissen wir, dass aus jedem Material eine Faser gewonnen, diese zu einem Textil, dann zu einem Produkt verarbeitet werden kann. Wenn Forschung und Design sich gemeinsam den dringenden Fragen der Zeit stellen und bereit sind, auf konventionelle, aus der Tradition entstandene Berufsdefinitionen und auf die oftmals hierarchischen Abfolgen in der Entwicklung und Lancierung von Produkten zu verzichten, können die Prozesse der Textilindustrie für Künftiges umgestaltet werden. Die Erfolge von jüngeren Firmen wie Freitag oder Qwstion, die sich seit ihrer Gründung mit der Materialentwicklung auseinandersetzen, um Produkte zu lancieren, die ihrer Vision und ihrem Verantwortungsbewusstsein als Gestalterinnen und Gestalter kompromisslos entsprechen, bekräftigen eine textile Zukunft der Schweiz.»

EVELYNE ROTH ist seit 2006 Dozentin für Kollektion und Oberflächengestaltung am Institut Mode-Design an der Hochschule für Gestaltung und Kunst FHNW in Basel. Für den Branchenverband Swiss Textiles setzt sie sich mit den aktuellen Trends und Innovationen im Bereich Textil auseinander und ist kreative Leiterin der Veranstaltung «Kontext».

"The liaison between fashion and textiles is a part of cultural history that may sometimes seem familiar and at other times more distant, but their interdependence has always been existential. Without textiles there can be no fashion, and without fashion there would be no transformative textile industry. Viewing them as two distinct design disciplines no longer corresponds to reality. Anyone developing products today needs to research materials, design surfaces, and think in terms of the circular economy. Designing means taking responsibility. But the focus of that responsibility is constantly changing in step with the sociocultural issues of the times. The resulting designs may have an extroverted and individualistic flair, be consciousness-raising and radically unfashionable, or even timeless. The latter is a phenomenon that of course could not be more fashionable. Whether Swiss textile design has a future both nationally and internationally depends on how today's players respond to the relevant trends and how they continue to finetune their company and product structure. We know from science that fiber can be extracted from virtually any material and then processed into a textile and further into a product. When research and design join forces to address the pressing issues of the day and are prepared to abandon the conventional occupational definitions based on tradition, as well as the pervasive hierarchies in the development and launch of products, textile industry processes can then be reconceived to face the future. The successes of younger companies such as Freitag and Qwstion, which have since their inception been developing materials enabling them to launch products that uncompromisingly express their vision and sense of responsibility as designers, point to a bright textile future for Switzerland."

EVELYNE ROTH has been a lecturer in collection and surface design at the Institute of Fashion Design, FHNW Academy of Art and Design in Basel since 2006. For the Swiss Textiles industry association, she researches the latest trends and innovations in the textile sector and is the creative director of the "Kontext" event.

Video: Museum für Gestaltung Zürich. Produktion/Production: schwarzpictures.com, Zürich

CALIDA

WE WANT A BETTER WORLD — Viktor & Rolf × CALIDA Capsule Collection, 2020. Photos: Petrovsky & Ramone

Das 1941 gegründete Schweizer Label verkauft weltweit Nacht- und Unterwäsche sowie Loungewear. In Kollaboration mit dem niederländischen Modehaus Viktor & Rolf geht das Unternehmen neue Wege. Unter dem Kollektionsmotto *We want a better world* investiert CALIDA in Nachhaltigkeit – die Wäsche ist kompostierbar, nach dem Cradle-to-Cradle-Prinzip gefertigt und hat High-Fashion-Charakter.

The Swiss label, founded in 1941, sells nightwear, underwear, and loungewear worldwide. In collaboration with the Dutch fashion house Viktor & Rolf, the company is now breaking new ground. Under the collection slogan "We want a better world," CALIDA is investing in sustainability with underwear that is compostable and manufactured according to the cradle-to-cradle principle and yet has a high-fashion look.

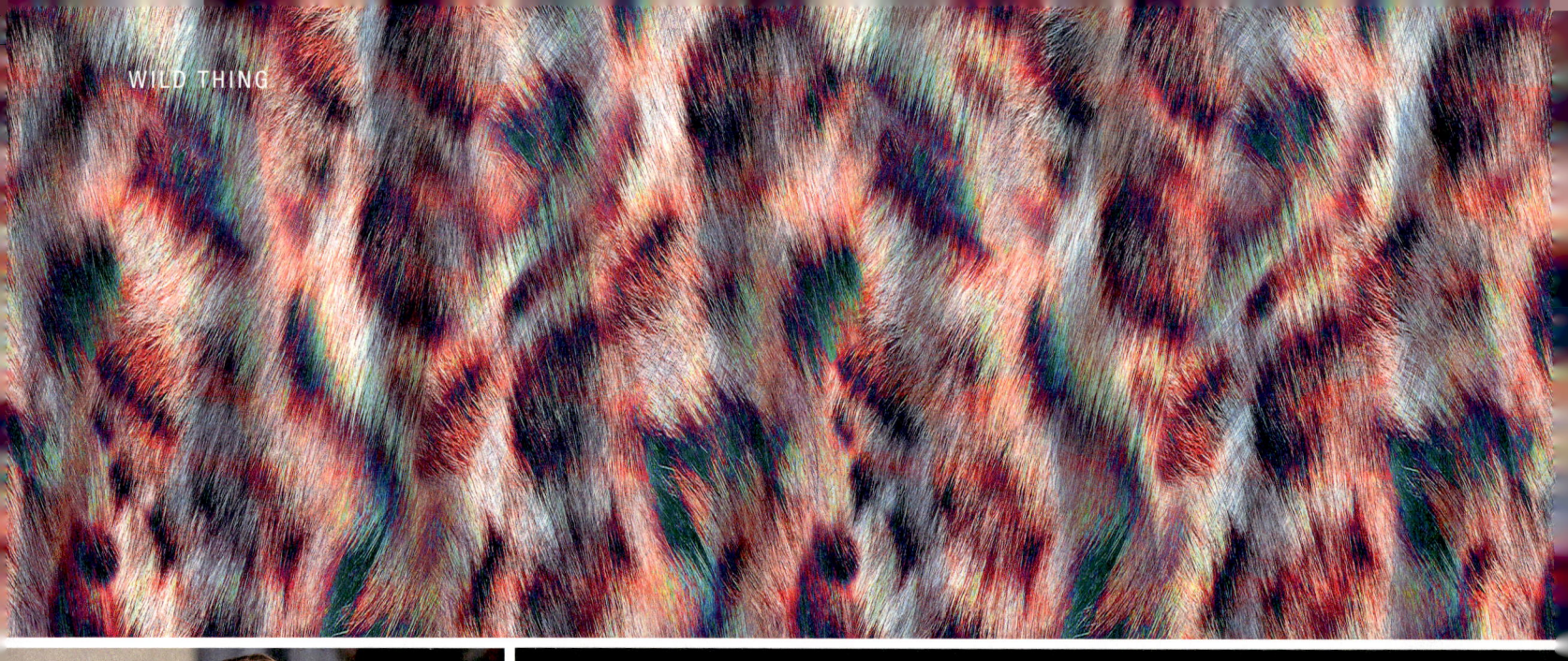

CLAUDIA CAVIEZEL

BUONA NOTTE, 2006 | linke Seite / left page | VIVIENNE WESTWOOD, Prêt-à-porter [im UZS / clockwise | 1: AW09/10. Stoff / Fabric: Jakob Schlaepfer AG, St. Gallen. Entwurf / Design: Claudia Caviezel; 2: AW11/12, Paris Fashion Week.
Photo: Stephane Cardinale / Corbis; 3: AW11/12. Stoff / Fabric: Jakob Schlaepfer AG, St. Gallen. Entwurf / Design: Claudia Caviezel; 4: AW09/10, Paris Fashion Week. Photo: Patrick Kovarik / AFP

Die Textilgestalterin Claudia Caviezel lernte ihr Handwerk an der Hochschule in Luzern. Nach mehrjähriger Tätigkeit als Designerin bei Jakob Schlaepfer arbeitete sie bis 2020 für Akris in St. Gallen. Daneben verfolgt sie bis heute eigene Projekte in den Bereichen Interieur, Architektur, Mode und Kunst. 2016 wurde sie mit dem Schweizer Grand Prix Design ausgezeichnet.

Textile designer Claudia Caviezel learned her trade at Lucerne University of Applied Sciences and Arts. After several years as a designer with Jakob Schlaepfer, she worked for Akris in St. Gallen until 2020. In parallel, she has continued to pursue her own projects in the fields of interior design, architecture, fashion, and art. Caviezel was awarded the Swiss Grand Prix Design in 2016.

CHRISTOPH HEFTI

WORLD MASK. 2014. Photo: Maniera | [linke Seite im UZS/left page, clockwise] 1: RING MY BELL. AW19, Julian Zigerli in Kollaboration mit/in collaboration with Christoph Hefti, 2019. Photo: Alexandre Haefeli; 2: MULTICOLOUR TIBETAN. 2015. Photo: Maniera; 3: TILE CARPET. 2019. Photo: Maniera; 4: NATURE (THE FIRST OR THE LAST DAY). 2018. Photo: Maniera

Christoph Hefti studierte Textildesign an der Hochschule für Gestaltung und Kunst in Zürich und Mode an der Central Saint Martins in London. Nach 13 Jahren als Creative Assistant bei Dries van Noten entwirft er freischaffend für Lanvin, Balenciaga, Acne Studios und Mugler. Nebenbei kreiert er limitierte, in Nepal hergestellte handgeknüpfte Teppiche.

Christoph Hefti studied textile design at Zurich University of the Arts and fashion at Central Saint Martins in London. After thirteen years as creative assistant to Dries van Noten, he designs freelance for Lanvin, Balenciaga, Acne Studios, and Mugler. On the side, Hefti also designs limited-edition hand-knotted carpets made in Nepal.

Bekannt geworden sind Markus und Daniel Freitag mit der Messenger Bag–1993 von Hand aus gebrauchten Lkw-Planen, Autogurten und Veloschläuchen genäht. 20 Jahre nach der ersten Tasche erweiterten sie das Angebot mit dem selbst entwickelten, kompostierbaren Textil «F-ABRIC».

Markus and Daniel Freitag became famous with the Messenger Bag they designed in 1993—sewn by hand out of used truck tarpaulins, seatbelts, and bicycle tubes. Twenty years after their first bag, they expanded the range with a self-developed compostable textile "F-ABRIC."

FREITAG

F-ABRIC Broken Twill aus Hanf und Leinen / Broken Twill of hemp and linen

LELA SCHERRER

[im UZS/clockwise] 1, 2: WIND TUNNEL GARMENTS. 2016. Photos: Jozo Palkovits;
3–6: KK COLLECTION. Photos: Andreas Zimmermann

Lela Scherrer gründete 2002 in Antwerpen und Basel ihr eigenes Studio für Mode- und Konzeptdesign. Ob als Design-Innovationsforscherin für Balenciaga oder als Designerin für Mode- und Interieurkollektionen – nebst ihren eigenen massgeschneiderten Kreationen setzt sie ihr Know-how vielseitig auch im Bereich von Bildung und Beratung ein.

Lela Scherrer opened her own studios for fashion and concept design in Antwerp and Basel in 2002. Whether working on design innovation research for Balenciaga or designing for fashion and interior collections, she applies her expertise to a variety of endeavors, including her own custom-made creations as well as consulting and training.

WILD THING

Das 2008 in Zürich gegründete Label setzt auf minimalistische Ästhetik und maximale Nachhaltigkeit. Für das Team um Christian Kägi, Matthias Graf und Hannes Schönegger ist die Entwicklung eigener Materialien der Schlüssel zu einer ökologisch sinnvollen Produktion. Aus Bio-Baumwolle oder Bananatex, dem weltweit ersten Textil aus Fasern der Bananenpflanze, stellen sie zeitlose Taschen her.

Founded in Zurich in 2008, the label is distinguished by a minimalist aesthetic and maximum sustainability. For the team around Christian Kägi, Matthias Graf, and Hannes Schönegger, developing their own materials is the key to an eco-friendly production. They make timeless bags from organic cotton or Bananatex, the world's first fabric made from banana fiber.

QWSTION BIOLIGHT COLLECTION, 2020. Photos: Yves Bachmann

QWSTION

FEMALE POWER — Es gibt Kleidung, Schuhe und Accessoires, die Stärke verleihen. Nach wie vor existiert in der Frauenmode ein klassischer Kleidercode, der sich an der Männerwelt mit ihren wertigen und langlebigen Stoffen und Schnitten orientiert: Ein Kostüm stattet die Trägerin mit Autorität und Würde aus. Welche Alternativen bietet Mode für die selbstbestimmte Frau? Und wo hört die gesellschaftliche Akzeptanz von stilistischen Extravaganzen auf? Das kreative Potenzial von Mode, die zu Empowerment führt, ist heute vorhanden. Wann wählen mehr Menschen ausgefallene Schnitte, gewagte Prints oder gar Leder für einen starken Auftritt?

FEMALE POWER

There are clothes, shoes, and accessories that make their wearers feel strong and confident. A classic dress code still exists in womenswear that is oriented on men's garments with their high-quality and enduring fabrics and cuts. Wearing a suit thus lends a woman an air of authority and dignity. But what alternatives does fashion offer the self-determined woman? And how much stylistic extravagance is still socially acceptable? Fashion today has plenty of creative potential for empowering women in different ways. When are more people going to opt for striking cuts, daring prints, or even leather to project a powerful impression?

«Mode ist ein Teil der Identität und Identität ist nie festgeschrieben, sie wird immer wieder neu aufgeführt und so auch umgestaltet.»

"Fashion is a part of identity, and identity is never fixed but is always performed anew and thus actually redesigned."

VIDEO — Katharina Tietze im Gespräch mit / in conversation with Christoph Hefti, 10/2020, 7 MIN.

KATHARINA TIETZE

«Wir können uns der Mode nicht entziehen. Mode ist Teil unseres Alltags, wir entscheiden jeden Morgen, was wir tragen, und kommunizieren damit etwas. Mode hat immer mit Abgrenzung und zugleich mit Anschluss zu tun. Wir sind gesellschaftliche Wesen und kleiden uns einerseits so, dass wir zu einer Gruppe dazugehören, andererseits streben wir Individualität an und möchten uns von der Gruppe abheben. Mode macht beides möglich.

Das Thema Gender ist für die Mode enorm wichtig. Die Männermode ist in den letzten Jahren vielfältiger und farbiger geworden, arbeitet heute mit interessanten Oberflächen. Sie hat also vermehrt feminine Aspekte adaptiert. Die Frauenmode macht das schon seit den 1920er-Jahren, seit Coco Chanel. Dieses Genderfluide der Gegenwart, das man zum Beispiel bei Gucci sehen kann, ist ein interessanter Spiegel der Gesellschaft und verweist auf die Fragen, mit denen sie sich beschäftigt. In der Mode zeigt sich das spielerisch oder provokant.

Mode ist ein Teil der Identität und Identität ist nie festgeschrieben, sie wird immer wieder neu aufgeführt und so auch umgestaltet. Damit verschieben sich auch die Codes der Mode permanent. Man kann das beispielhaft an einzelnen Elementen der Kleidung beobachten: Der Absatz hatte ursprünglich die Funktion, den Stiefel im Steigbügel zu halten. Dann wurde er zum modischen Accessoire und war lange den Frauen vorbehalten. Jetzt sieht man Absätze ab und zu auch bei Männern. Die Zuschreibungen verschieben sich also ständig, und jeder kann aktiv daran mitwirken. Das ist das Utopische und Lustvolle an der Mode.»

KATHARINA TIETZE ist Professorin für Design an der Zürcher Hochschule der Künste und leitet dort die Fachrichtung Trends & Identity. Als ausgebildete Bekleidungsdesignerin war sie Kostümbildnerin am Theaterhaus Jena, später Mitarbeiterin am Lehrstuhl Moden und öffentliche Erscheinungsbilder an der Bauhaus-Universität Weimar. Sie forscht zum Thema Mode im Spannungsfeld von Stil und Alltagskultur.

"We cannot really escape fashion. It is a part of our daily lives. Every morning, we all decide what to wear, and we use clothes to communicate something. Fashion always has to do with distinction as well as commonality. We are social beings: so on the one hand we dress in order to belong to a group; on the other hand we want to distinguish ourselves and be individuals. Fashion actually makes both things possible.

The issue of gender is extremely important in fashion. This has become very obvious in recent years, as men's fashion has become more diverse and colorful, working with interesting textures. It has adapted more and more feminine aspects. Women's fashion has been doing this for a long time — since the 1920s, since Coco Chanel. This gender fluid element of the present — which shows up, for example, in the Gucci collections — is an interesting reflection of society and the questions our society is dealing with. In fashion, this manifests itself in a playful or provocative way.

Fashion is a part of identity, and identity is never fixed but is always performed anew and thus actually redesigned. And in this respect, fashion codes are constantly shifting. You can actually observe this in individual pieces of clothing: for example, the heel was originally invented to anchor boots into stirrups. At some point it became a fashion accessory, and was reserved for women for a long time. Now you can sometimes see heels for men. So the attributions keep changing, and everyone can play an active part in this. This is the utopian and exciting part of fashion."

KATHARINA TIETZE is professor for design and head of the Trends & Identity department at Zurich University of the Arts. A trained fashion designer, she worked as a costume designer at the Theaterhaus Jena and later in the Department of Fashion, Trend & Public Appearance at the Bauhaus University in Weimar. Tietze conducts research on fashion at the crossroads between style and everyday culture.

Video: Museum für Gestaltung Zürich. Produktion / Production: schwarzpictures.com, Zürich

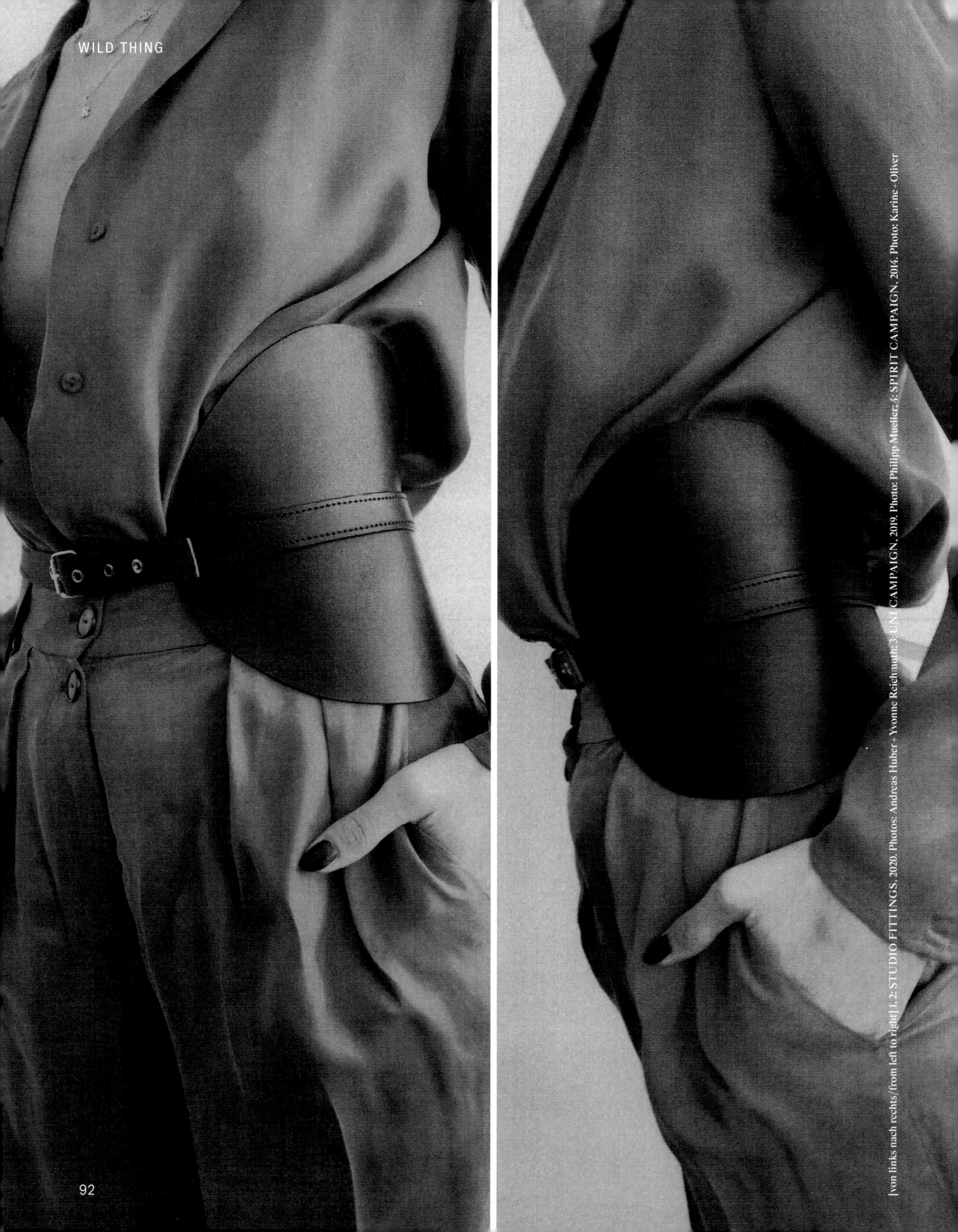

[von links nach rechts/from left to right] 1, 2: STUDIO FITTINGS. 2020. Photos: Andreas Huber + Yvonne Reichmuth; 3: UNI CAMPAIGN. 2019. Photo: Philipp Mueller; 4: SPIRIT CAMPAIGN. 2014. Photo: Karine + Oliver

YVY

Yvonne Reichmuth ist ausgebildete Modedesigne-rin, in Florenz erlernte sie das Sattler-Handwerk. Seit 2013 entwirft sie mit ihrem Label YVY exquisite Lederaccessoires, die zwischen Lingerie, Schmuck und Kleidung changieren und für Frauen wie für Männer gedacht sind. 2019 wurde das Label mit dem Design Preis Schweiz geehrt.

Yvonne Reichmuth has a degree in fashion design and also learned the saddler's trade in Florence. Since 2013 she has been designing exquisite leather accessories under her YVY label. Her product line encompasses lingerie, jewelry, and clothing and is intended for both women and men. The label was awarded the Design Prize Swit-zerland in 2019.

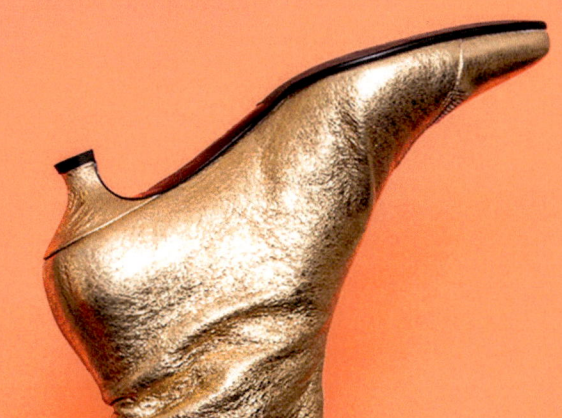

Die gelernte Schuhmacherin und Designerin Stefi Talman entwirft seit über 40 Jahren Schuhe und Accessoires aus Leder. Bekannt wurde sie 1979 mit dem bis heute produzierten Modell ZIP—einer Bottine ohne Absatz, aus weichem Leder und mit schräg eingesetztem Reissverschluss. Mit Talman erlebte der Schuh 1980 die Zürcher Jugendunruhen, den Post-Punk und New Wave.

Stefi Talman, who trained as a shoemaker and designer, has been designing leather shoes and accessories for over forty years. She rose to fame in 1979 with her ZIP boot, which is still in production today—a heelless ankle boot made of soft leather with a diagonal zipper. Together with Talman, the boot witnessed the Zurich youth riots in 1980 and the post-punk and New Wave eras.

[von oben nach unten/from top to bottom] ZIP, 1980. Photo: Felix Schregenberger; PIZ, AW19/20. Photo: Rita Palanikumar | [rechte Seite/right page] Pumps DUE, Schnürschuhe/Lace-up shoes FOR, AW11/12. Photo: Rita Palanikumar

STEFI TALMAN

Unter dem legendären Label Thema Selection entwirft und verkauft Sissi Zoebeli Mode in der Zürcher Altstadt. Gut geschnittene Frauenkleider aus teuren, langlebigen Stoffen, die wie ein klassischer Herrenanzug für Status und Stil stehen, sind seit den späten 1980er-Jahren ihr Markenzeichen. Thema Selection bringt pro Jahr nur zwei Kollektionen mit 12 bis 15 Stücken heraus.

Sissi Zoebeli has been designing and selling fashion in Zurich's Old Town under the legendary label Thema Selection. Well-cut women's dresses made of costly and durable fabrics that convey the same kind of status and style as a man's suit have been her trademark since the late 1980s. Thema Selection produces only two collections of twelve to fifteen pieces per year.

Smokingjacke und Hose/Tuxedo jacket and trousers. 1980. Model: Irene. Photo: Sissi Zoebeli | [rechte Seite/right page] Irene für/for Thema Selection, 1981. Photo: Sissi Zoebeli

THEMA SELECTION

KOLLEKTION/COLLECTION 2020. Photos: Marianne Mueller

OUTDOOR — Kleidung funktioniert als Schutzschicht zwischen Körper und Umgebung. Bilder hochalpiner Extremszenarien zeigen in Daunen verpackte Michelin-Menschen. In den Augen von Städtern wirken diese topmodisch. Dick wattierte und abgesteppte Hüllen finden deshalb trotz wärmer werdender Winter auch in niederen Lagen begeisterte Träger. Denn ob im urbanen Kontext oder in der freien Wildnis: Sich uneingeschränkt von Wind und Wetter zu bewegen, gilt als neuer Luxus. Nur ein schmaler Grat trennt Outdoor-Wear von Mode. Da werden Wärmeschichten üppig und bunt aufgetragen, Fellstiefel sehen aus wie Pferdefüsse und ein Glarner Strickpullover vertreibt die bösen Geister.

OUTDOOR

Clothing functions as a protective layer between the body and the environment. Pictures of extreme high-alpine scenarios often show "Michelin Men" swaddled in down. To city-dwellers, they look very fashionable. Thick padding and quilted sleeves are therefore happily donned even in lower altitudes, despite winters that are getting warmer. Because whether in an urban setting or the great outdoors, being able to move around freely in wind and weather is seen as a new form of luxury. There is a fine line between outdoor wear and fashion, for example warm layers built up lavishly in bright colors, fur boots modeled on horse's hooves, or a knitted sweater from Glarus that purportedly wards off evil spirits.

Der markante, an japanische Ästhetik angelehnte Stil, die Farbe Schwarz und Performances statt Modeschauen machten die charismatische Designerin Christa de Carouge in Zürich zu einer Ikone mit treuer Anhängerschaft. Seit 2015 entwickelt die Nachfolgerin Deniz Ayfer unter dem Label DE NIZ die Couture-Stücke für zeitgenössische Nomadinnen weiter.

Her distinctive style, based on Japanese aesthetics, the color black, and performances instead of fashion shows, has made the charismatic designer Christa de Carouge an icon with a loyal following in Zurich. Since 2015, Carouge's successor Deniz Ayfer has been carrying on the production of couture pieces for contemporary nomadic women under the label DE NIZ.

URBAN NOMAD, 1998, Christa de Carouge. Photo: Erick Julia | [linke Seite im UZS/left page, clockwise] 1, 2, 4, 5: Jacke MOHANG | Jacket MOHANG mit Schal, Oberteil DRAGON mit überlangen plissierten Stulpen, Hose ROSA/Jacket MOHANG with scarf, top DRAGON with extra long pleated sleeves, trousers ROSA; 3, 6: Jacke SOLEIL PAPILLON, Oberteil TUNIKA mit Schlitz und überlangen Ärmeln, Hose SUPER CLOWN/Jacket SOLEIL PAPILLON, Top TUNIKA with slit and extra long sleeves, trousers SUPER CLOWN. Photos: Deniz Ayfer

DE NIZ

JULIAN ZIGERLI

RING MY BELL, AW19, Julian Zigerli in Zusammenarbeit mit/in collaboration with Christoph Hefti, 2019. Photos: Alexandre Haefeli

Nachdem Julian Zigerli an der Universität der Künste Berlin Modedesign studierte, gründete er 2011 in seiner Heimat Zürich ein eigenes Label. Wilde Prints, ein frisches Männerbild und künstlerische Kollaborationen sind Merkmale seiner Arbeit. Die Herbstkollektion 2019, die mit Motiven der Schweizer Volkskunst spielt, entstand in Zusammenarbeit mit dem Designer Christoph Hefti.

Julian Zigerli studied fashion design at Berlin University of the Arts and then founded his own label in his hometown of Zurich in 2011. Wild prints, a fresh take on menswear, and artistic collaborations are the hallmarks of his designs. The autumn collection 2019, which plays with motifs of Swiss folk art, was created in collaboration with the designer Christoph Hefti.

KANDAHAR / KDH1932

Das 2020 lancierte Label KDH1932 bringt 18 exklusive Schuhmodelle heraus. Es sind auf Bestellung angefertigte Einzelstücke, die in der Schuhmanufaktur Kandahar am Thunersee hergestellt werden. Damit sucht die Traditionsmarke Kontakt zu einem jungen modeaffinen Publikum. Wer die Klassiker kennt, liest die extravaganten Modelle als einen humorvollen Gruss.

The KDH1932 label, launched in 2020, offers eighteen exclusive shoe designs. They are one-of-a-kind pieces made to order and produced in the Kandahar shoe manufactory on Lake Thun. With this new line, the tradition-steeped brand is courting a young, fashion-forward clientele. Those who are familiar with the classics will see in these extravagant shoes a humorous nod to the past.

Das 1862 gegründete Unternehmen mit Sitz in Seon (AG) stellt hochwertige Funktionsbekleidung mit minimalem ökologischem Fussabdruck her. Das Sortiment ist divers und reicht vom Seil über die Lawinenschaufel bis hin zu Kleidung für den alpinen Extremsport. Trendige, performative Hüllen – Schlafsack oder Jacke – sprechen auch modebewusste Städterinnen und Städter an.

Founded in 1862 and based in Seon (AG), Mammut produces high-quality functional wear with a minimal carbon footprint. The product line is diverse, ranging from ropes and avalanche shovels to clothing for extreme alpine sports. Trendy, high-performance cover-ups – whether sleeping bags or jackets – also appeal to the fashion-conscious city dweller.

Where will you sleep next? 2019 Photos: Lukas Wassmann/WATCHSOME GmbH + MAMMUT

[1m UZS/clockwise] 1–3 MAMMUT RECOVERY SERIES. Schlafsack/Sleeping bag RELAX. PROTECT. PERFOR. RECOVERY SERIES. Schlafsack/Sleeping bag PROTECT. Photo: Mammut Sports Group AG

MAMMUT

1969 gründete Kurt Ulmer in St. Moritz die Luxusmarke JET SET. Mit bunten Textildrucken und starken Farben revolutionierte er die Skimode der 1980er-Jahre. Aktuell lenkt der Kreativdirektor Michael Michalsky das Label von Berlin aus. Im Zürcher Archiv findet er die Inspirationen für den frischen Mix aus moderner Funktionalität und luxuriösem Streetstyle.

The luxury brand JET SET, founded by Kurt Ulmer in St. Moritz in 1969, revolutionized ski fashion in the 1980s with colorful printed fabrics and intense hues. Currently, creative director Michael Michalsky is managing the label from his base in Berlin. The brand's Zurich archive is a fertile source of inspiration for a fresh mix of modern functionality and deluxe street style.

AW19/20. Photos: Daniela Müller-Brunke

JET SET

WILD THING

Die 1851 in Schönenwerd (SO) gegründete Firma Bally blickt auf eine lange Tradition in der Produktion hochwertiger Schuhe zurück. Ihre Kreativabteilung operiert heute im Luxussegment von Mailand aus. Aktuell erfahren Klassiker aus dem Firmenarchiv ein zeitgenössisches Revival: Seit je stand das Label für innovative Funktionsschuhe in den Bereichen Berg- und Wintersport.

Founded in 1851 in Schönenwerd (SO), Bally can look back on a long tradition of producing high-quality shoes. The company's creative division is today based in Milan, operating in the luxury fashion sector. Classics from the company archives are currently experiencing a revival, which is hardly surprising as the label has always been a byword for innovative functional footwear in the field of alpine and winter sports.

BALLY

108

BALLY PEAK OUTLOOK CAPSULE COLLECTION. 2020. Photo: Michel Comte

MINIMAL — MAXIMAL — Lange galten in der Mode verbindliche Regeln — ein Kanon, wo etwas üppig aufgebauscht oder wo es einfach und verhalten auszufallen hatte. Aktuell existieren minimalistische Ästhetik und Konzepte, die auf ein Maximum zielen, nebeneinander. Mit Stoff, Schnitt, Farbe und Muster wird eine Opulenz gefeiert, deren Anblick schlicht überwältigt und verzaubert. Oder aber es wird nach der reduzierten Form gesucht, vernünftig mit den materiellen Ressourcen umgegangen und dem Detail besondere Beachtung geschenkt. Beim Minimalismus geht es nicht um den Zauber der Reichhaltigkeit, sondern um das Staunen angesichts sichtbarer Qualität und der Tatsache, wie einfach alles sein kann.

MINIMAL—MAXIMAL

Fashion was long governed by binding rules, a canon for when something should look lavishly exaggerated or simple and restrained. Today, minimalist aesthetics exist side by side with concepts that aim for maximum impact. Fabric, cut, color, and pattern may unleash an exuberant feast for the eyes, while in other cases the goal is a reduced form, handling material resources sensibly, or paying special attention to detail. Minimalism is not about enchantment but about marveling at tangible quality and just how simple things can be.

«Das ist eigenartig und ein ungelöster Widerspruch in diesem Land: dass es die Stoffe hin zum Maximalismus gezogen hat, die Designer aber eher die Kunst des Weglassens kultiviert haben.»

"This is a little strange, and it is an unresolved contradiction in this country: the fabrics tended towards maximalism, but the designers rather cultivated the art of omission."

VIDEO — Jeroen van Rooijen im Gespräch mit / in conversation with Christoph Hefti, 10/2020, 6 MIN.

JEROEN VAN ROOIJEN

«Die Mode schwingt stets zwischen Minimalismus und Maximalismus hin und her. Einmal ist sie sehr laut und deutlich, grell und überzeichnet, dann wieder minimalistisch, puristisch, sec und reduziert. Diese Hin-und-her-Bewegungen sind typisch und entsprechen sicher auch der Lust der Konsumenten. Zumindest in den letzten 75 Jahren hat es diese beiden Richtungen tatsächlich immer gegeben. Sie drängen sich gegenseitig nie ganz ab. Und das ist auch gut so, es gilt die ganze Bandbreite der Kundschaft zu bedienen.

Es gibt jene Minimalisten, die es maximal auf die Spitze treiben, die das Weglassen so weit perfektionieren, dass nichts mehr weggelassen werden kann. Eine solche Kleidung ist formal und äusserlich minimal, aber im Bemühen ist sie maximal. Andererseits gibt es eine Kleidung, die in ihrem Ausdruck extrem ist, aber nicht in ihren Zutaten. Mit wenigen Mitteln oder Schnitten, vielleicht sogar nur mit ein paar guten Handgriffen wird eine maximale Wirkung erzielt. Die beiden Prinzipien können also Hand in Hand gehen, sie können sich sogar potenzieren.

Der minimalistische Grundton in der Schweiz steht auch ein bisschen im Widerstreit mit der Textilbranche, die zumindest in den letzten 60 Jahren doch auch bekannt war für ihre Ausdrucksstärke. Die Produkte der St. Galler Firmen oder auch der Zürcher Seidenindustrie waren meist Stoffe mit viel Reichtum. Das ist eigenartig und ein ungelöster Widerspruch in diesem Land: dass es die Stoffe hin zum Maximalismus gezogen hat, die Designer aber eher die Kunst des Weglassens kultiviert haben.»

JEROEN VAN ROOIJEN ist gelernter Modegestalter und selbstständiger Journalist. Er schreibt unter anderem für die Neue Zürcher Zeitung, Annabelle, Bolero oder GQ zu den Themen Mode und Stil. Während seiner langjährigen Tätigkeit beim NZZ-Verlag baute er das Stilressort auf und lancierte die Luxus-Beilage Z. Er ist Mitinhaber des Concept Stores Cabinet im Viadukt in Zürich.

"Fashion keeps oscillating between minimalism and maximalism. Sometimes everything has to be very loud and clear, garish and exaggerated; then it becomes minimalist, purist, sober, and reduced again. These are typical swings of the pendulum, and certainly also reflect the consumers' wishes. As far as the last seventy-five years of fashion history are concerned, these two trends have indeed always existed. They never crowd each other out entirely. And that's a good thing: it is important to serve the entire range of customers.

There are those minimalists who really push their minimalism to the max: they perfect omission to such an extent that you simply can't cut out anything else anymore. This kind of clothing is, formally and externally, minimalist; but in terms of effort, it is maximalist. On the other hand, there is clothing that is extreme in its outward expression, but not in its ingredients. By minimal means or simple cuts—perhaps just a few well-placed touches—maximum effect is achieved. Both principles can go hand in hand and even intensify each other.

In a way, this prevailing minimalist tone in Switzerland is somewhat in conflict with the country's textile industry, which, at least for the last sixty years, has been known for its expressiveness. The fabrics produced by the St. Gallen companies or the Zurich silk industry were very luxurious. This is a little strange, and it is an unresolved contradiction in this country: the fabrics tended towards maximalism, but the designers rather cultivated the art of omission."

JEROEN VAN ROOIJEN, who has a degree in fashion design, works as a freelance fashion and style journalist for periodicals including the Neue Zürcher Zeitung, Annabelle, Bolero, and GQ. During his many years at the newspaper NZZ, he built up the style department and launched the luxury supplement "Z." Van Rooijen is co-owner of the Cabinet concept store in one of Zurich's Viadukt arches.

Video: Museum für Gestaltung Zürich. Produktion / Production: schwarzpictures.com, Zürich

AMORPHOSE

Kollektion AW 19, 2019, Photo: Giancarlo Bello | rechte Seite | rechte Seite im UZS; right page, clockwise 1, 2: Kollektion AW20, 2020; 3: BONBON, SS21 s-TIGER, SS21. Photos: Alexander Palacios

Giancarlo Bello kreiert mit seinem Label amorphose voluminöse Couture-Mode. In Florenz ausgebildet, vertiefte er seine Kenntnisse zunächst in italienischen Modehäusern und machte sich 2007 in Lugano selbstständig. Verspielte Details wie Rüschenkragen, ungewöhnliche Textilkombinationen und Farborgien in Orangerot sind Merkmale seiner skulpturalen Kreationen.

Giancarlo Bello creates voluminous couture fashions under his label amorphose. Trained in Florence, he honed his skills working for Italian fashion houses and then set up his own business in Lugano in 2007. Playful details such as ruffled collars, unusual fabric mixes, and color orgies in orange-red are typical features of his sculptural creations.

VELT

An der Hochschule für Gestaltung und Kunst FHNW in Basel zu Produktdesignern ausgebildet, entwirft das Zürcher Designerduo Stefan Rechsteiner und Patrick Rüegg heute minimalistische Lederschuhe und -accessoires in Berlin. Die Produktion erfolgt in einer kleinen Schuhmanufaktur in Othmarsingen im Kanton Aargau und in Budapest, Ungarn. 2013 erhielt Velt für die Debut Kollektion und 2016 für die Entwicklung einer verstellbaren Sohle den Schweizer Designpreis.

After completing their degrees in product design at the FHNW Academy of Art and Design in Basel, the Zurich designer duo Stefan Rechsteiner and Patrick Rüegg now design minimalist leather shoes and accessories in Berlin. The items are produced by a small shoe manufactory in Othmarsingen in the canton of Aargau, and in Budapest, Hungary. Velt received the Swiss Design Award in 2013 for its Debut Collection and in 2016 for its development of an adjustable sole.

[im UZS/ clockwise] 1: CLAUDIA BERTINI/ SHOW 2. Einladungskarte/ Invitation card. Photo: Claudia Bertini; 2.3: LOOKBOOK 3; LOOKBOOK 6. Photos: Andrea Diglas

CLAUDIA BERTINI

Claudia Bertini entwirft in Zürich mit edlen italienischen Stoffen, sucht eine klare Linienführung und überrascht dann und wann mit applizierten Details. 2018 stellte sie im Rahmen des Vogue Salon in Berlin aus. Die neusten Modelle ihrer fortlaufenden Kollektion präsentiert sie zusammen mit befreundeten Kunstschaffenden an Pop-up-Events.

Zurich designer Claudia Bertini designs garments in sumptuous Italian fabrics whose clean lines are sometimes unexpectedly interrupted by appliquéd details. She exhibited at the Vogue Salon in Berlin in 2018. Bertini presents the latest designs from her growing collection at pop-up events together with her artist friends.

SONNHILD KESTLER

ELEFANTENDRACHEN. 2018 | [linke Seite/left page] FIGUREN UND FORMEN. Allover, 2020. Photos: Arthur David

Sonnhild Kestler studierte Textildesign in Zürich und betreibt dort seit über 30 Jahren ihr eigenes Siebdruckatelier. Inspiration für ihre bunten Drucke findet sie auf Reisen, in der Folk Art aus Mittelasien, Indien, Südamerika und Osteuropa oder in der Handwerkskunst. Die Motive überträgt sie auf Kleidung, Foulards, Kissen und Teppiche. 2010 wurde Kestler mit dem Schweizer Grand Prix Design ausgezeichnet.

Sonnhild Kestler studied textile design in Zurich and has been running her own screen printing studio there for over thirty years. She finds inspiration for her colorful prints on her travels, in folk art from Central Asia, India, South America, or Eastern Europe, and in traditional handicrafts. The motifs are then used on clothing, silk scarves, cushions, and carpets. Kestler was awarded the Swiss Grand Prix Design in 2010.

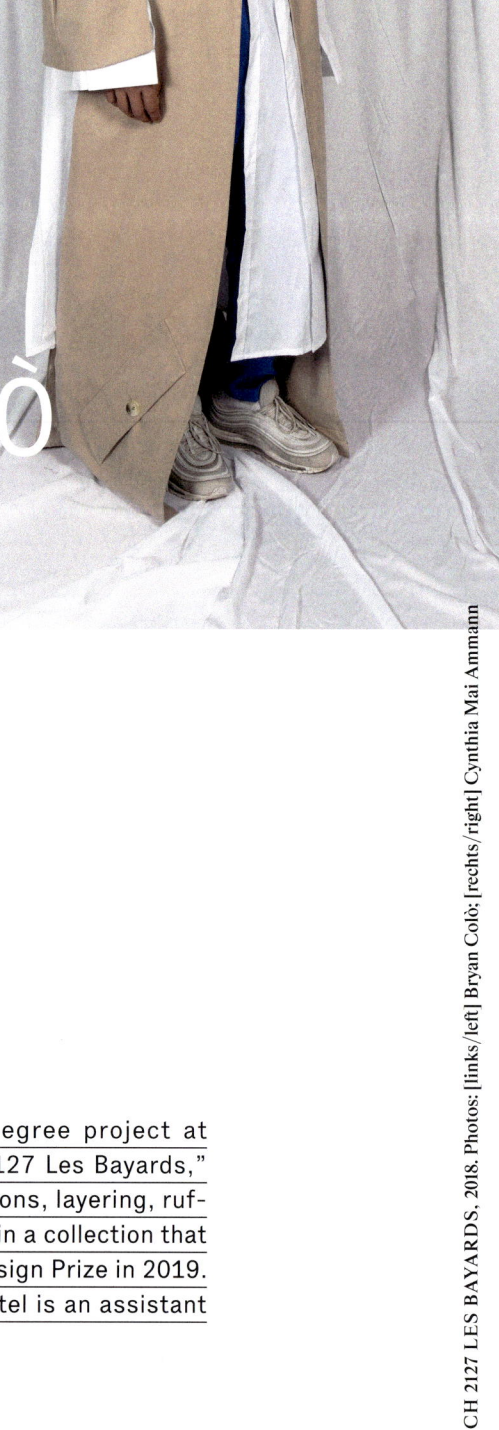

BRYAN COLÒ

CH 2127 LES BAYARDS. 2018. Photos: [links/left] Bryan Colò; [rechts/right] Cynthia Mai Ammann

Bryan Colò studierte an der HEAD–Genève. In seiner Bachelorarbeit *CH 2127 Les Bayards* treffen Oversize-Schnitte, ungewöhnliche Proportionen, Layerings, Rüschen und Fransen aufeinander. Die Abschlusskollektion wurde 2019 für den Schweizer Designpreis nominiert. Zurzeit assistiert der gebürtige Neuenburger als Stylist bei Celine in Paris.

In Bryan Colò's bachelor's degree project at HEAD–Genève, entitled "CH 2127 Les Bayards," oversize cuts, unusual proportions, layering, ruffles, and fringes come together in a collection that was nominated for the Swiss Design Prize in 2019. Currently, the native of Neuchâtel is an assistant stylist at Celine in Paris.

FAMILY MATTERS — Mode ist Lifestyle. Dieses Prinzip begreift Foulards, Kissen, Tassen oder Kleider als ein einziges modisches Universum, das seinerseits einer ästhetischen, gesellschaftlichen oder politischen Haltung entspringt. Familien — auch soziale — sind ein ideales Biotop für diese Spielart der Mode. Sie stiften Identität und Sinn. Kundinnen und Kunden, Freundinnen und Freunde sind Teil dieser Familie, man trifft sich im Ladengeschäft. Das Schaufenster spiegelt die Marke. Der entsprechende Style funktioniert als visuelles Wiedererkennungsmerkmal und bestätigt, dass man geschmacklich richtig liegt und gesellschaftlich dazugehört.

FAMILY MATTERS

Fashion is lifestyle. This means that silk scarves, cushions, mugs, or dresses may form a stylistic universe all their own, born of an aesthetic, social, or political attitude. Families — as well as close-knit social groups — are an ideal biotope for this variety of fashion, which can lend people a sense of identity and meaningfulness. Customers, friends, and relatives are all part of the family, meeting up at the shop, where the display window telegraphs the brand. The style then fosters brand recognition and reaffirms that one has good taste and belongs to the crowd.

etmoietmoi, NUAGE weiss. Photo: Florian Lauber; Janine Grubenmann, MOVE YOUR LINE, 2020/21. Photo: tobias-siebrecht.com ||linke Seite im UZS/left page, clockwise|1: Blueberry, Wolljacke/Wool jacket, AW20/21. Photo: Lucia Ferretti; 2: K | Rosenberg, Schultertasche klein/Shoulder bag small, 2020. Photo: Christoph Walther; 3: foulalà, SOUND OF FOREST skin, 2020; 4: foulalà, PARADISO pink, 2020. Photos: foulalà

TOKU SWISS LABELS

2009 eröffneten Mariann Lammerskitten und Zimi Kesselring den Laden TOKU swiss labels. In der Berner Altstadt vereinen sie ausgesuchte Schweizer Labels unter einem Dach. Aktuell sind dies die Strickmanufakturen erfolg, xess + baba und Beige sowie die Marken Mademoiselle L und etmoietmoi. Nur die Holzsandalen liess TOKU swiss labels unter eigenem Label produzieren.

Mariann Lammerskitten and Zimi Kesselring opened the shop TOKU swiss labels in 2009. They bring selected Swiss labels together under one roof at their location in Bern's Old Town. Current labels include the knitwear makers erfolg, xess + baba, and Beige, as well as the brands Mademoiselle L and etmoietmoi. TOKU swiss labels only produced its wooden sandals under its own label.

ENSOIE

1974 rief Monique Meier das auf bedruckte Seide spezialisierte Label ins Leben. 40 Jahre später übernahmen die drei Töchter Anna, Sophie und Eleonore den Familienbetrieb in Zürich. Die Produktpalette reicht heute von Keramik über Kleidung bis hin zu Accessoires. Der unverkennbare Stil äussert sich in der Kombination von Handwerk und Glamour.

Monique Meier created this label specializing in printed silk in 1974. Forty years later, her three daughters Anna, Sophie, and Eleonore took over the family business in Zurich. The product range today extends from ceramics to clothing and accessories. The distinctive style consists of an appealing blend of craftsmanship and glamour.

WILD THING

Guya Marini und Carmen D'Appollonio fertigen seit 2006 kunstvolle Einzelstücke und Kleinserien. Nach dem Modestudium in Berlin arbeitete Marini zunächst als freischaffende Designerin und Stylistin, während D'Appollonio dem Künstler Urs Fischer assistierte. Heute lebt Marini in Zürich, D'Appollonio in Los Angeles. Ihr ikonisches Stück ist das mit Recycling-Schnur umhäkelte Foulard.

Guya Marini and Carmen D'Appollonio have been producing artful one-of-a-kind pieces and small series since 2006. After studying fashion in Berlin, Marini first worked as a freelance designer and stylist, while D'Appollonio assisted the artist Urs Fischer. Today Marini lives in Zurich and D'Appollonio in Los Angeles. Their iconic piece is a silk scarf with a crocheted border made of recycled string.

[im UZS / clockwise] 1. 3.: N°21, 2020. Photo: Christian Knörr + Helvetia Leal; 2.: N°20, 2019. Photo: Flavio Karrer | [rechte Seite / right page] N°21, 2020. Photo: Sara Merz

IKOU TSCHÜSS

VIDEO — Mode Suisse Captured, Edition 15, Migros Museum für Gegenwartskunst Zürich, 02/2019, 17 MIN.

MODE SUISSE

Seit bald 20 Editionen verkörpert die *Mode Suisse* eine dynamische Plattform zur Promotion von Schweizer Modedesign. Mit feinem Gespür für die wichtigsten Tendenzen der Modeszene wählt eine Fachjury Saison für Saison Schweizer Designerinnen und Designer für eine Teilnahme aus. Sie bietet Formate wie Laufsteg, Showroom und Paneldiskussionen, die Sichtbarkeit und Präsenz in einem hart umkämpften Markt generieren. Durch die halbjährlichen Editionen ermöglicht die *Mode Suisse* den Labels den professionellen Austausch und die Zusammenarbeit mit dem Einzelhandel, den Medien, der Textilindustrie und anderen Akteurinnen und Akteuren der Branche. Vorwiegend in Zürich und Genf durchgeführt, agiert sie seit 2014 auch international mit Veranstaltungen in Peking, Mailand und London sowie mit dem *DACH Showroom Paris* und *Swiss Touch Presents: Mode Suisse at NY Fashion Week*.

Seit knapp zehn Jahren ist die *Mode Suisse* vor allem für das Entdecken junger vielversprechender Talente bekannt. Durch ihre Fördertätigkeit trug sie zu den Erfolgsgeschichten von beispielsweise Rafael Kouto, Julia Heuer, Kévin Germanier, Julian Zigerli, Nina Yuun, After Work Studio, Garnison und YVY bei. Die Zusammenarbeit mit jungen Talenten ist ihr ebenso ein Anliegen wie die kontinuierliche Unterstützung etablierter Designerinnen und Designer sowie Schweizer Kulturschaffender, die etwa in den letzten beiden grossen Shows von Christa de Carouge, einer für den Laufsteg kuratierten Lesung von Arno Camenisch oder der musikalischen Begleitung durch Greg Haines sichtbar wird.

Organisiert und choreografiert wird die *Mode Suisse* durch das Team um Initiator Yannick Aellen, zu dem unter anderem Ejra Sunna und Lina Eisenhut gehören. *Mode Suisse* wird massgeblich von Engagement Migros, der Zürcherischen Seidenindustrie Gesellschaft (ZSIG), der Hulda und Gustav Zumsteg-Stiftung und der Schweizer Kulturstiftung Pro Helvetia getragen.

Over the course of almost twenty editions, *Mode Suisse* has proven to be a dynamic platform for the promotion of Swiss fashion design. Season after season, a jury of experts selects Swiss designers to participate based on a keen understanding of the central trends shaping the fashion scene. *Mode Suisse* offers formats including catwalks, showrooms, and panel discussions in an effort to generate greater visibility and presence for Swiss fashion in a highly competitive market. The semi-annual editions give labels an opportunity to engage in professional exchanges and collaborations with retailers, the media, the textile industry, and other stakeholders in the sector. Usually operating in Zurich and Geneva, *Mode Suisse* began expanding to the international arena in 2014 with events in Beijing, Milan, and London, as well as the *DACH Showroom Paris* and *Swiss Touch Presents: Mode Suisse at NY Fashion Week*.

For almost ten years now, *Mode Suisse* has been known primarily for discovering promising young talent. Its promotional activities helped launch the success stories of designers and labels including Rafael Kouto, Julia Heuer, Kévin Germanier, Julian Zigerli, Nina Yuun, After Work Studio, Garnison, and YVY. Besides working with young talents, however, *Mode Suisse* also provides ongoing support for established designers and Swiss cultural players, as is evident from the last two major shows by Christa de Carouge, a reading by Arno Camenisch curated for the catwalk and a musical score composed by Greg Haines.

Mode Suisse is organized and choreographed by initiator Yannick Aellen and his team, whose members include Ejra Sunna and Lina Eisenhut. The main sponsors are Engagement Migros, the Zurich Silk Association (ZSIG), the Hulda and Gustav Zumsteg Foundation, and the Swiss Arts Council Pro Helvetia.

After Work Studio, Mode Suisse Edition 17. 2020. Photo: Johanna Hullar | [linke Seite oben/left page, top] Video: Mode Suisse. Idee und Konzept/Idea and concept: Tsitaliya Mircheva. Produktion/Production: Andi Caplazi; [linke Seite unten/left page, bottom] Jacqueline Loekito, Mode Suisse Edition 14. 2018. Photo: Eduard Meltzer

«Ich wurde in eine richtige Textilindustriefamilie hineingeboren. Der Familienbetrieb, eine Seidenweberei, die ab den 1930er-Jahren auch eine Filiale in England unterhielt, existiert seit fast 200 Jahren. Ich bin 1964 in die Firma eingetreten und konnte in diesem Beruf meine Leidenschaft für Textilien voll entfalten.

Die Schweizer Mode hat mich immer schon interessiert, auch als ich noch im Textilverband aktiv mitgewirkt habe. Neben dem Flaggschiff Akris gab es sehr viele Talente, auch deshalb haben wir uns im Verband damals überlegt: Wie kann man – auch im Interesse der hiesigen Textilindustrie – die Schweizer Mode fördern? Wir suchten also nach einem Projekt, das Schweizer Textilien national und international bekannt machen kann.

Im Jahr 2000 schufen wir den mit 100 000 Euro dotierten *Swiss Textiles Award*. Er wurde zunächst im Rahmen der *Gwand* in Luzern verliehen, später in Zürich. Die *Gwand* war 1992 von Suzanna Vock ins Leben gerufen worden, später stiess Yannick Aellen dazu. Sie haben zusammen mit dem Schweizer Textilverband Grosses geleistet. Unter den Ausgezeichneten war 2003 der damals noch wenig bekannte Raf Simons, ein Jahr später gewann Haider Ackermann und 2009 Alexander Wang. Innerhalb von zehn Jahren wurde der *Swiss Textiles Award* zum weltweit renommiertesten Modeförderpreis.

Als Reaktion auf die einbrechenden Umsätze in der Modebranche musste die Schweizer Textilindustrie umstrukturieren. Sie hat auf technische, innovative Textilien umgestellt und dabei die Modebranche sukzessive etwas vernachlässigt. Das war auch das Ende des *Swiss Textiles Award*, der 2010 zum letzten Mal verliehen wurde.

RONALD WEISBROD

"I was born into a real textile-industry family. The family business, a silk weaving mill, has existed for almost 200 years and also had a branch in England from the 1930s onward. I joined the company in 1964 and was able to fully develop my passion for textiles in this profession.

I had always been interested in Swiss fashion, also when I was actively involved in the Swiss Textile Association. In addition to the flagship label, Akris, there were many other gifted designers. This was one reason why we in the association wondered: how can Swiss fashion be promoted, particularly in the interest of the local Swiss textile industry? So we were looking for a project that would make Swiss textiles known nationally and internationally.

In 2000 we created the *Swiss Textiles Award*, endowed with 100,000 euros. It was first presented at the *Gwand* in Lucerne, and later in Zurich. The *Gwand* was founded in 1992 by Suzanna Vock, who was later joined by Yannick Aellen. Together with the Swiss Textile Association, they have achieved great things. Among the award winners in 2003 was Raf Simons, who was still little known at the time; Haider Ackermann won the award one year later, and Alexander Wang received it in 2009. Over the course of ten years, the *Swiss Textiles Award* became the world's most prestigious fashion promotion prize.

However, in reaction to a drop in sales, the Swiss textile industry had to restructure extensively. Its focus moved toward technological, innovative textiles, and it gradually neglected the fashion industry. That was also the end of the award: it was presented for the last time in 2010.

Früher gab es vielleicht 50 Betriebe für Kleiderstoffe, heute kann man sie an einer Hand abzählen. Für Modedesignerinnen und -designer ist es schwierig geworden, in der Schweiz die richtigen Partner zu finden. Es wird auch keine grosse Palette mehr produziert. Aber jene Firmen, die noch aktiv sind, möchten, dass die Schweizer Modeindustrie weiterhin Bestand hat. Deshalb hat sich die Zürcherische Seidenindustrie Gesellschaft dazu entschlossen, die *Mode Suisse* zu fördern. Sie ist eine ideale Plattform, die es Schweizer Modeschöpferinnen und -schöpfern erlaubt, auf sich aufmerksam zu machen. Und das ist ihrem Gründer Yannick Aellen gelungen.

Die Zürcher Seidenindustriellen waren immer schon die modeaffinsten unter den Schweizer Textilherstellenden, so macht Modeförderung Sinn für uns. Denn auch wenn junge Schweizer Designerinnen und Designer heute mit ausländischen Textilien arbeiten, ist es wichtig, sie zu unterstützen. Die Schweizer Textilmode soll die Möglichkeit behalten, auf sich und ihre Talente aufmerksam zu machen.»

RONALD WEISBROD wurde in eine Familie geboren, die seit 1825 Textilien – zunächst Seide – herstellte und vertrieb. In England aufgewachsen, stieg Ronald Weisbrod in den 1960er-Jahren in den Familienbetrieb ein. Er führte die Firma durch prosperierende Jahre wie auch durch Krisenzeiten. 2012 musste die Produktion in Hausen am Albis stillgelegt werden.

VIDEO — Ronald Weisbrod im Gespräch mit / in conversation with Karin Gimmi, 10/2020, 15 MIN.

Video: Museum für Gestaltung Zürich. Produktion/Production: schwarzpictures.com, Zürich

There used to be some fifty companies producing clothing fabrics in Switzerland; today, just a handful are left. It has become difficult for fashion designers to find the right partners here. The industry no longer produces such a broad range. But those who do still manufacture textiles want the Swiss fashion industry to remain alive. That's why the Zurich Silk Association decided to support *Mode Suisse*. It is the ideal platform that allows Swiss fashion designers to make themselves known. And its founder, Yannick Aellen, has succeeded in doing so.

Zurich's silk industrialists have always been the most fashion-conscious among Swiss textile manufacturers; that's why fashion promotion makes sense to us. Even if young designers nowadays work with textiles from other countries, it's important to support them. Swiss fashion designers should still have opportunities to draw attention to themselves and to their products."

RONALD WEISBROD was born into a family that had been manufacturing and selling textiles — initially silk — since 1825. Raised in England, he joined the family business in the 1960s. Weisbrod went on to steer the company through years of both prosperity and crisis until the production lines in Hausen am Albis finally had to shut down in 2012.

VIDEO — F+F Diplompräsentation / Diploma presentation, 2020, 9 MIN.

F + F ZURICH

[linke Seite im UZS/left page, clockwise] 1: Video: F+F Schule für Kunst und Design Zürich; 2: Diplompräsentation/Diploma presentation Backstage, 2020. Photo: Pamela Castillo; 3: Projekt/Project CATWALK im/at Atelier Hermann Haller; SLAVIZITÄT, Kreation/Design Vladislav Alexander Rieger, 2020.

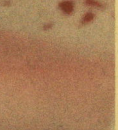

«Man könnte ketzerisch behaupten, es brauche keine Mode mehr. Wenn Designerinnen und Designer schlagartig aufhören würden, zu entwerfen, wenn keine Mode mehr produziert werden würde, gäbe es noch immer ausreichend Kleider. Die Welt würde weiterfunktionieren. In diesem Kontext erwarten wir von unseren Studierenden, dass sie verantwortungsvoll denken und dass sie das, was sie machen, begründen. Es geht nicht mehr nur darum, schöne Kleider zu entwerfen. Sie sollen überzeugende Konzepte erarbeiten.

Dabei ist es uns wichtig, den Austausch mit anverwandten Disziplinen wie Kunst, Film, Fotografie oder visuelle Gestaltung zu fördern. Zum einen werden sie später mit Fotografen, Gestaltern oder Künstlern direkt zusammenarbeiten, zum anderen stärkt diese Begegnung die Auseinandersetzung mit der eigenen Disziplin und zeigt auch deren Grenzen auf.

Unsere Dozierenden sind nicht nur Lehrerinnen und Lehrer, sie arbeiten als Künstlerinnen, als Designer, als Modezeichnerinnen. Die Studierenden profitieren so nicht nur von fachlichem Know-how und langjähriger Erfahrung, sondern auch von dem, was wir aus unserer Arbeitswelt in den Unterricht tragen. Das ist ein wechselseitiger Austausch: Die Arbeit mit den Studierenden fordert auch die Dozierenden dazu auf, gestalterische Positionen oder etablierte Verarbeitungsmethoden stets neu zu hinterfragen.

Provokation, radikale Experimente und das Infragestellen des Vorhandenen gehören dazu. Wir fördern gestalterischen Mut und das Ausloten von Grenzen: ‹Lehnt euch so weit aus dem Fenster, dass ihr euch beinahe vor euch selbst erschreckt!›

Natürlich wünschen wir uns, dass die Studierenden diese Art des Denkens auch nach ihrem Abschluss weiterverfolgen. Gerade bei internationalen Labels ist diese Fähigkeit ausgesprochen gefragt. Wenn sie hingegen ihr eigenes Label gründen, müssen sie einen idealen Mittelweg finden zwischen Kommerzialität und dem Bedürfnis, die gestalterische Identität zu wahren.»

Nicole Schmidt und Heiner Wiedemann,
Studiengangsleitung Modedesign

"One might quite heretically claim that fashion is no longer necessary. If all designers suddenly stopped designing, if fashion were no longer produced, there would still be enough clothes. The world would not stop working. In this context, we expect our students to think responsibly and to justify what they do. It's no longer just about making beautiful clothes. They must develop convincing concepts.

It is important to us to encourage an exchange with related fields such as art, film, photography, or visual design. First of all, they will later collaborate with photographers, designers, or artists; secondly, these encounters strengthen the examination of their own discipline and also demonstrate its limits.

Our lecturers are not only teachers; they also work as artists, designers, or fashion illustrators. Students thus benefit not only from our professional know-how and many years of experience, but also from what we bring from our professional work into the classroom. This is a reciprocal exchange: working with students also challenges lecturers to constantly question their creative positions or established working methods.

Provocation, radical experiments, and questioning the status quo are part of it. We support creative courage and exploring boundaries: 'Go out on a limb so far that you almost scare yourselves!'

Of course, we want our students to follow through with this way of thinking after their studies are over. Especially with international labels, it is precisely this ability that is required of them. If they start their own labels, they will need to find an ideal balance between commercial success and the need to preserve their identities as designers."

Nicole Schmidt and Heiner Wiedemann,
Co-Directors, Fashion Design

VIDEO — Doing Fashion Graduation, Institut Mode-Design, Hochschule für Gestaltung und Kunst FHNW in Basel / Institute of Fashion Design, FHNW Academy of Art and Design in Basel, 2020, 21 MIN.

HGK FHNW IN BASEL

[linke Seite oben/left page, top] Videostills DOING FASHION GRADUATION, 2020 [im UZS/clockwise] Anastasia Bull; Selina Hirsch; Reto Emmenegger; Mara Danz; [linke Seite unten/left page, bottom] DON'T BELT UP. UNSTRAP YOURSELF!, 2020. Model: PriskA*MORger. Bodypainting: Eva Buehler. Photo: Yasmina Haddad

DON'T BELT UP. UNSTRAP YOURSELF!

«Meine holistische Arbeit ist die Erscheinung meiner gelebten Erfahrungen. Meine sanfte Zunge spricht: Mir gefällt es, ins Licht des Beobachters zu sehen, denn ich selbst bin Beobachterin. Das Gefühl der Ungleichheit als Frau in der Gesellschaft begann bereits in meiner Kindheit aufgrund meiner camouflierten Haut Vitiligo. Es war eine Art stiller Dialog mit einem lauten Blick durch den verkörperten Stil—eine Aura, die für sich selbst spricht.

Seither bin ich auf einer Soul-Promenade, um einer neuen, unbekannten Perspektive, einem anderen Bewusstsein bezüglich Körper, Seele und Schönheit Ausdruck zu verschaffen, kurz: um die Ungleichheit zu kultivieren. In diesem Sinne initiierte ich im Jahr 2011 unser Credo der *doing fashion look therapy*:

Die Herausforderung, die Gleichförmigkeit zu überwinden, kann nur von denjenigen angepackt werden, die Mode im erweiterten, holistischen Sinne kurieren.

Der Körper unter den Lederhautgürteln eröffnet sich und klopft an die Tür:
—GÜRTEL 1, ein Leitmotiv: Schnallt alle eure Gürtel enger und wählt den, den euer Innerstes öffnet.
—GÜRTEL 2, ein Problem: Die Einförmigkeit und die Massenproduktion des Modesystems sind dem Untergang geweiht.
—GÜRTEL 3, ein Aufruf: Unterstützt die ungleiche Diversität unserer Körper.
—GÜRTEL 4, ein Wunsch: Kommt zusammen, um pulsierende, funkelnde und kreative emotionale Formate zu erschaffen.
—GÜRTEL 5, Hoffnung: Ändert das System, um es der ungleichen Diversität unserer Körper anzupassen und um kreative ‹Spass de Luxe›-Zeit zu verbringen. Psychohygiene versus Psychoterror.
—GÜRTEL 6, ein Impuls: Keine Reisen mit vorgezeichneten Körpern und Normierungen. Aktiviert euren Esprit und häutet euch von Konventionen.
—GÜRTEL 7, ein Ausblick: Tragt eure Herzen und eure Augen stolz auf der Zunge.
—GÜRTEL 8, eine Aktion: *Don't belt up. Unstrap yourself!*»

DON'T BELT UP. UNSTRAP YOURSELF!

"My holistic work is the manifestation of my experiences. My gentle tongue begins to speak: I like to see the light of the observer, because I am an observer myself. As a woman I started feeling the inequality in society as early as my childhood due to my skin patterned by vitiligo. It was a kind of silent dialogue with a loud gaze through the embodied style—an aura that speaks for itself.

Since then I've been on a soul promenade aiming to offer a new expressive perspective, a new awareness of body and beauty—in short, to foster the inequality. With this in mind, I developed our credo of *doing fashion look therapy* in 2011:

The challenge of overcoming uniformity can only be met by those who heal fashion in an extended holistic sense.

The body beneath the belts is revealed and manifests itself:
—BELT 1, a leitmotif: Buckle all your belts tighter and choose the one that opens your innermost self.
—BELT 2, an issue: The uniformity and mass production of the fashion system are doomed.
—BELT 3, a demand: Foster the inequality of our bodies.
—BELT 4, a wish: Come together to create vibrating, sparkling, and creative emotional formats.
—BELT 5, a hope: Change the system to fit our individual bodies and spend 'Spass de Luxe' time. Mental hygiene versus psychological terror.
—BELT 6, an impulse: No travel with prerecorded bodies and norms. Activate your esprit and defy conventions.
—BELT 7, an outlook: Wear your hearts and your eyes proudly on your tongue.
—BELT 8, an action: *Don't belt up. Unstrap yourself!*"

Seit 2011 ist PriskA*MORger künstlerische Leiterin und Professorin am Institut Mode-Design, Hochschule für Gestaltung und Kunst FHNW in Basel.

Since 2011, PriskA*MORger has been creative director and professor at the Institute of Fashion Design, FHNW Academy of Art and Design in Basel.

VIDEO — Défilé HEAD, 2019, 29 MIN.

HEAD — GENÈVE